Common Core
Writing Handbook

GRADE

6

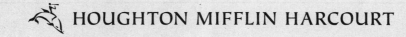

HOUGHTON MIFFLIN HARCOURT

Copyright © by Houghton Mifflin Harcourt Publishing Company

Printed in the U.S.A.

ISBN 978-0-547-86454-9

20 21 22 23 24 0982 21 20 19 18 17 16

4500611793   C D E F G

Contents

How to Use This Book 6

Purposes for Writing 8

The Writing Process 10

The Writing Traits 12

Writing Forms Narrative Writing

    Lesson 1: Personal Narrative Paragraph 14

    Lesson 2: Personal Narrative 16

    Lesson 3: Story Scene 18

    Lesson 4: Fictional Narrative: Prewriting 20

    Lesson 5: Fictional Narrative:

        Drafting/Revising 22

  Argument Writing

    Lesson 6: Response Paragraph 24

    Lesson 7: Argument Paragraph 26

    Lesson 8: Book Review 28

    Lesson 9: Argument: Prewriting 30

    Lesson 10: Argument: Drafting/Revising 32

  Informative Writing

    Lesson 11: Procedural Essay 34

    Lesson 12: Classification Essay 36

    Lesson 13: Definition Essay 38

    Lesson 14: Informational Essay: Prewriting 40

    Lesson 15: Informational Essay:

        Drafting/Revising 42

  Informative Writing

    Lesson 16: Compare-Contrast Essay 44

    Lesson 17: Problem-Solution Essay 46

    Lesson 18: Cause-Effect Essay 48

    Lesson 19: Research Report: Prewriting 50

    Lesson 20: Research Report: Drafting/Revising . 52

  Argument Writing

    Lesson 21: Opinion Essay 54

    Lesson 22: Problem-Solution Essay 56

    Lesson 23: Persuasive Letter 58

    Lesson 24: Argument: Prewriting 60

    Lesson 25: Argument: Drafting/Revising 62

Contents

Narrative Writing

    Lesson 26: Narrative Poem 64

    Lesson 27: Field Notes 66

    Lesson 28: Radio Script 68

    Lesson 29: Personal Narrative: Prewriting 70

    Lesson 30: Personal Narrative:

        Drafting/Revising 72

Writing Strategies The Writing Process

    Prewriting 74

    Drafting 76

    Revising 78

    Editing 80

    Publishing 81

    Writing Traits

    Ideas : 82

    Organization 84

    Voice 86

    Word Choice 87

    Sentence Fluency 88

    Conventions 90

    Writing Workshop 92

Technology Using the Internet 94

    Writing for the Web 96

Research Doing Research 98

    Notetaking 100

Test Prep Writing to a Prompt 102

Evaluation Checklists and Rubrics 104

Writing Models and Forms Informative Writing

    Cause-Effect Essay 106

    Problem-Solution Essay 108

    Compare-Contrast Essay 110

    How-to Essay 112

Explanation Essay 114

Classification Essay. 116

Definition Essay 118

Interview. 120

News Story 122

Survey: Social Studies 123

Business Letter 124

Science Observation Report 125

Research Report. 126

Graphs, Diagrams, and Charts 128

Multimedia Presentation 130

Narrative Writing

Personal Narrative. 132

Biography. 134

Fictional Narrative. 136

Fantasy Story 138

Play 140

Opinion Writing

Opinion Essay. 142

Persuasive Essay. 144

Response to a Play. 146

Author Response 148

Book Review 150

Persuasive Speech 152

Practical Writing

Notetaking Strategies. 154

Journal 156

Index 158

How to Use This Book

Writing is a great tool. It can help you solve problems as well as express yourself. For example, you can use it to nail down an idea or hammer out a point. This handbook will help you discover ways to use this tool well.

What Is a Handbook?

If writing is a tool, then this handbook is the how-to manual. It contains clear definitions, strategies, models, and key practice. Refer to its pages as much as you need to before, during, and after writing.

Sections of This Book

This handbook has three sections:

 Writing Forms—Definitions, labels, and models of key writing forms

 Writing Strategies—Ideas and methods that you can use for every kind of writing

Writing Models and Forms—Models of good writing

How to Find Information

Find information in this book in two different ways:

- **Use the contents page.** Find the section you need, and then turn to the entry that most closely matches the topic you want.
- **Use the tabs at the top of left-hand pages.** The names of the tabs change with each section. You can flip to sections that interest you to skim and scan for the information that you seek.

Purposes for Writing

A blank page can be intimidating. Luckily, there are many ways to overcome the blank page. One way to plan your writing before you start is to think about your **purpose**, or your main reason for writing. You can determine your purpose by asking yourself, *Why will I write?*

● To Inform

To inform means to share or show information. Sometimes it is meant to instruct or teach. Sometimes it relates interesting facts or details. Some kinds of informative writing are articles, reports, and essays.

● To Explain

To explain means to tell about a topic by describing *what, why,* and *how.* You can explain a topic in any type of writing. Some examples of writing to explain are instructions, science observation reports, and explanations.

● To Narrate

To narrate means to tell a true or fictional story. You might write to amuse, touch, or thrill your reader. You might also write to express thoughts and feelings. Some kinds of writing to narrate are short stories, novels, and personal narratives.

● To Persuade

To persuade means to convince someone else to agree with your opinion or to take action. Examples of writing to persuade include a letter, a speech, an argument, or a review.

Understanding Task, Audience, and Purpose (TAP)

In addition to choosing a purpose for writing, you should consider your **audience**, or for whom you are writing. For example, you might write differently when writing to a friend than when writing to someone you don't know. Think about who will be reading your writing as you plan.

Finally, choose a **task**, or writing form. For example, if you want to persuade your class to do something, you might write a speech, an essay, or make a poster.

Before you begin writing, it is a good idea to decide your task, audience, and purpose, or **TAP**. You may choose your own TAP, or your TAP may be assigned to you.

Ask yourself these questions.

Task: What kind of writing will I do?

Do I want to write a poem, a story, a research report, or something else?

Audience: Who will read my writing?

Am I writing for a teacher, a friend, a committee, or someone else?

Purpose: Why am I writing?

Am I writing to inform, explain, narrate, or persuade?

The Writing Process

Writing can be like taking a journey through your own imagination. You begin with a destination in mind, but the road you take to get there may not be direct. As you travel, you sometimes make discoveries that lead you in new directions. There is no right or wrong road, but the writing process provides a map to guide you.

As you write, you may choose to exit to another stage in the writing process before continuing. You may choose the same exit more than once. You may pass an exit and return to it later. It's your choice—you, the writer, are in the driver's seat.

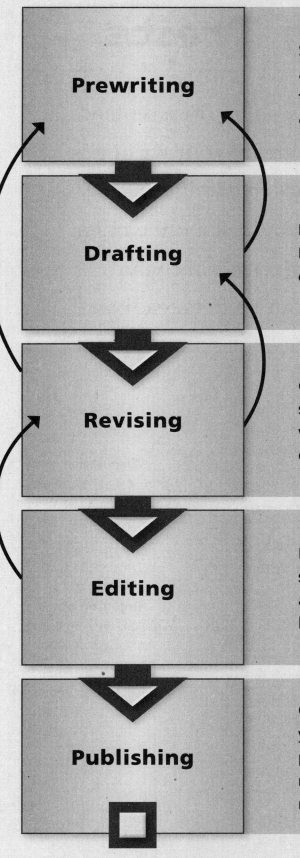

Prewriting

Start with your TAP—task, audience, and purpose. Then choose a topic that fits your TAP. Gather and organize information about the topic.

Drafting

Put your ideas into a first draft. Don't worry about your errors. You can fix them later.

Revising

Go back and read your writing to see if it meets your purpose. Meet with a partner or small group to discuss it.

Editing

Now is the time to correct any spelling, grammar, usage, mechanics, and capitalization errors you may have made.

Publishing

Consider how you want to publish your work. Some possibilities are posters, group presentations, multimedia presentations, and oral reports. Share your writing.

The Writing Traits

Good writing keeps you reading from sentence to sentence. How can you tell if your writing is good? All good writing has five traits, or characteristics. Once you understand the traits, you'll know what to look for to make your writing great and keep your readers reading.

Conventions
Correct punctuation, grammar, and spelling

Evidence
Details and ideas that develop a topic

Elaboration
Precise and descriptive language that makes writing interesting

The Traits of Good Writing

Purpose
A writer's reason for writing

Organization
Writing is well organized and easy to follow

Development
Vivid characters, setting, and events that create an interesting story

Traits Checklist

As you practice writing, ask yourself these questions.

☑ **Evidence**	Do I explain ideas with details and examples? Do I support opinions with facts and details?
☑ **Organization**	Do I have a strong beginning? Are my details organized logically? Do I have a strong ending?
☑ **Purpose**	Is my reason for writing clear? Does my tone make me seem interested in my topic?
☑ **Elaboration**	Did I use vivid and precise words and phrases to develop my topic or tell a story?
☑ **Development**	Did I include details that help readers visualize the characters and settings? Did I tell the story events in an interesting way?
☑ **Conventions**	Are my spelling, grammar, capitalization, and punctuation correct?

Personal Narrative Paragraph

A **personal narrative paragraph** is a narrative about an experience from the writer's own life told from the first-person, "I," point of view.

Parts of a Personal Narrative Paragraph

- An opening sentence to introduce the topic and grab the reader's attention
- Details and actions presented in logical order
- Details that explain thoughts and feelings about the event, using the word "I"
- Vivid descriptions to help the reader picture what happened

Beginning
Grabs the reader's attention

Events
Actions in time order

Vivid Details
Show what happened and how the author felt

Ending
Shows the author's reaction to the event

My heart raced when our teacher announced the rules for the writing contest. I'd always wanted to be a professional writer, but I'd never told anyone because I didn't think I was good enough. This was my chance to prove myself and have my own story published in a literary journal. I went straight home **after** school and got to work. I already knew exactly what I wanted to write about. The characters seemed to be **flying out of my head,** and I couldn't write fast enough. I finished my final draft just **before** Dad made me go to bed. **My mind jumped** between excitement and worry. I knew it was my best story yet, but was it good enough? Did I have any chance at all? My **hands shook** when I turned in the manuscript the next morning. I didn't know how I could wait an entire week to find out if I had won. When the day **finally** came, I couldn't focus in class or eat anything at lunch. My fingers rapidly tapped the top of the desk at the beginning of 6th period **while** I sat waiting for the announcement. When the principal's crackling voice said my name over the PA system, I could have jumped as high as the ceiling. Perhaps I had what it took to become a writer after all.

Other Transitions
First
Later
Eventually
After
Next
Following

Name _____

Follow your teacher's directions to complete this page.

We Do 1

My favorite day at school was when _____

_____. First, _____

_____.

Then, _____

_____

_____

_____.

The best part was _____

_____

_____

_____

_____

_____.

Eventually _____

_____

_____

_____.

You Do 2

On a separate sheet of paper, write a personal narrative paragraph about a time when you got to do something exciting.

You Do 3

On a separate sheet of paper, use your prewriting plan to write a personal narrative paragraph, or make a new plan that tells about a time when you were afraid.

Personal Narrative

A **personal narrative** describes an event or theme in the life of the writer. It explains why that event is important.

Parts of a Personal Narrative

- A clear beginning, middle, and end to the story
- Details about how the writer felt during the events and how the writer felt afterward
- An ending that shows the story's importance to the writer

Beginning
Grabs the reader's attention

I used to hate practicing music. My mother made me take piano lessons every Saturday morning starting when I was eight. My little brother was allowed to stay home watching cartoons, but I had to go to Mrs. Finklestein's and learn the piano. Sometimes I would pretend to be sick, but that didn't work too well. "If you're too sick for piano, then you're too sick to go out and play," said my mother. So I went to Mrs. Finklestein's.

Details
Show thoughts and feelings

It wasn't that I didn't like music. I *loved* music. But I didn't love the music I had to play on the piano. There was so much counting! On the piano, I had to count every beat, and I had no control over the sound. I could bang a piano key loudly or tap it quietly, but I couldn't change if it sounded pretty or angry or sad. Also, our piano was old, so most of the notes sounded dull except the F-sharp, which didn't sound at all.

Everything changed last October when my mom put on an old jazz record. I loved it! Every note sounded different, and I couldn't predict what would happen next. My mom said the musician was Miles Davis, and he played the trumpet.

Other Transitions
First
Next
Later
Then
Also

Ending
Tells how the reader felt about what happened

Well guess what? Now I play the trumpet in the school band. And I love practicing music!

Name _____

Follow your teacher's directions to complete this page.

We Do 1

Lots of holidays are special, but my favorite holiday was when I _____

_____.

This is because _____.

_____

_____

_____

Even better, _____

_____

_____

_____

The best part was _____

_____

_____

_____

_____

_____

_____

_____

Lots of holidays are great, but this one was the best... until next year!

You Do 2

On a separate sheet of paper, write a personal narrative about a time when you lost something.

You Do 3

On a separate sheet of paper, use your prewriting plan to write a personal narrative, or make a new plan to tell about a time you did something that made you proud.

Story Scene

A **story scene** is a brief fictional narrative of one event that is part of a longer story.

Parts of a Story Scene

- Opening that introduces characters and setting
- Parts of the plot
- Events told in order
- Details and dialogue bring the scene to life

Beginning
Introduces characters and setting

"That should do it." Jakob sighed as he added the last tiny piece to his model of the Colosseum. After weeks of painstaking work, his social studies project was finally done.

"Jakob!" **hollered** Maia, "Dinner!" His door opened.

"No!" Jakob **yelled,** vaulting across his room. "No one is allowed in until I take my Colosseum to school!"

"But I want to see," Maia whined.

Middle
Describes events in time order

"Absolutely not!" Jakob **said.** Ignoring his sister's protests, he closed the door and headed downstairs.

Jakob returned to his room after dinner. He froze when he saw his door open a tiny crack.

"MAIA!" Jakob's voice exploded through the house. He was horrified to find the model covered with drawings of miniature people.

"Do you like it?" Maia grinned from the door. "The Colosseum was a type of theatre, right? And every theatre needs an audience."

Dialogue and Description
Bring characters and actions to life

Jakob's head fell into his hands. The project was due tomorrow, so there was no time to cover over the drawings. He glared at his little sister, but her bright eyes slowly melted away his remaining anger. At least there was no real damage done.

"Well, I guess they are kind of appropriate," he **admitted.** "I just hope Mrs. Dasho has a sense of humor."

Other Dialogue Tags
Grumbled
Suggested
Whispered
Sang
Asked
Wondered

Name _____

Follow your teacher's directions to complete this page.

1 The bright noon sun _____

_____. Soon it was _____

_____.

_____

_____. Suddenly _____

_____.

_____

_____

_____. It was clear that _____

_____

_____

_____.

Without a doubt _____

_____

_____

_____.

2 On a separate sheet of paper, write a story scene that uses mostly dialogue.

3 On a separate sheet of paper, use your prewriting plan to write a story scene, or make a new plan that describes a different scene.

Fictional Narrative: Prewriting

A **fictional narrative** is an imaginative story with characters and a plot. It has a beginning, a middle, and an ending.

Parts of a Fictional Narrative

- A plot with events told in sequential, or time, order
- A setting, or when and where the story takes place
- A problem, or conflict, that the characters must solve
- An ending, or resolution, that wraps up the story

Title: Andrew Wants a Pet

Setting: current day, Andrew's room	**Characters:** Andrew, talking pet goldfish

Plot

Problem (Conflict): Andrew wants a pet, but his house is too small for a dog and his mom is allergic to cats.

Events: Andrew wishes for a bigger house, and his fish grants the wish. Andrew doesn't like cleaning the big house, so his fish makes it smaller again. Andrew wishes away his mom's cat allergy, but then he is allergic to cats.

Ending (Resolution): Andrew is satisfied with having a talking fish for a pet.

Name _____

Follow your teacher's directions to complete this page.

 1 **Title:** The Lamp

Setting: a yard sale, Aviva's house	**Characters:** Aviva

Plot

Problem (Conflict):

Events:

Ending (Resolution):

 2 On a separate sheet of paper, complete a story map for a fictional narrative about a kid who finds a time machine.

 3 On a separate sheet of paper, plan a fictional narrative about something strange that happens to an ordinary kid.

Fictional Narrative

A **fictional narrative** is an imaginative story with characters and a plot. It has a beginning, a middle, and an ending.

Parts of a Fictional Narrative

- A plot that is usually told in time order, or sequence
- Details and dialogue that make the events and characters seem real
- A conflict, or problem, that the characters must solve
- A climax, or high point, that shows how the characters solve the problem
- An ending that wraps up the story

Beginning
Introduces the characters, setting, and problem

Middle
Contains details and dialogue that make characters seem real

Climax
Shows how the character solves the problem

Ending
Wraps up the story

Andrew wanted a pet more than anything. His mother told him that their house was too small for a dog, and she was allergic to cats. All Andrew had was a goldfish in a glass bowl.

Alone in his room with his fish, Andrew muttered, "I wish our house were bigger!" **Suddenly**, it was. In fact, it was huge!

"Be careful what you wish for," the goldfish said. As much as Andrew wanted a dog, his chore—vacuuming—would have taken all of his time and energy.

"Okay, I wish the house were small again," he told the goldfish. **Right away**, the house changed back.

"One more wish, you foolish boy," the goldfish warned.

"Okay," Andrew said, "I wish my mom weren't allergic to cats!" **The next day**, Andrew brought home a cat. His mother was fine, but Andrew started to sneeze and couldn't stop. He had to give the cat to a friend. **At last,** he gave up.

"All right, you win," he told the fish. "No more wishes. I guess a fish that talks isn't the worst pet in the world!"

Other Transitions
At first
After a while
During
Later
Before long
Finally
In the end

Name _____

Follow your teacher's directions to complete this page.

1 Aviva never thought she would have an adventure—until the day she found the strange-looking lamp at a yard sale. She brought it home and rubbed it with a cloth. Suddenly _____

_____

_____.

Right away, _____

_____

_____. The next day, _____

_____

_____.

Later on, _____

_____

_____

_____. Before long, _____

_____

_____

_____. In the end, _____

_____

_____

2 On a separate sheet of paper, write a fictional narrative about a character who finds a time machine.

3 On a separate sheet of paper, use your prewriting plan to write a fictional narrative, or plan and write a story about something strange that happens to an ordinary kid.

Response Paragraph

A **response paragraph** tells how the writer feels about a piece of literature that he or she has read. The writer interprets the work and draws a conclusion about it.

Parts of a Response Paragraph

- An opening that clearly states the writer's main idea about the original text
- A brief summary of the characters, setting, and plot
- Examples and quotations from the text
- A closing that restates the writer's idea and connects the text to the writer's own life

Opening Sentence
States the writer's main idea or opinion

Summary
Tells writer's opinions about the characters, setting, and plot

Examples and quotations

Closing
Restates the main idea

Rudyard Kipling's *Kim* is an adventure story, but it is also a story about growing up and finding out who you are. **The story is about** Kim, an Irish orphan living in Lahore, India. Kim joins a monk on a spiritual journey because Kim wants to learn from him. As they travel, Kim is taken from the monk and educated in a British school. At school, he becomes a British spy. **Then** he graduates and reunites with the monk. They journey to the Himalayan Mountains. They are both hurt in an exciting battle with French and Russian spies. Luckily, Kim gets important maps from the spies. **After** Kim and the monk get better, Kim helps the monk reach his goal. Through these adventures, Kim discovers that he is "a mixture o' things." He is not completely Indian and not completely British. Like Kim, I am a mixture of things. I am like my father in some ways and like my mother in others. I also have my own interests and feelings. Kim has an exciting life in a faraway country, but we are alike because we have to find our true selves.

Other Words for Responding
In the book
The plot starts
The first thing
Next
The best part
One similarity
In my opinion

Name _____

Follow your teacher's directions to complete this page.

"Science Friction," by David Lubar, is a very funny story. _____

_____

_____. The story is about_____

_____

_____

_____

_____. Then _____

_____

_____

_____

_____. After _____

_____

_____

_____. I think_____

_____

_____

_____

_____

_____

On a separate sheet of paper, write a response paragraph about a book, story, or play that inspired you. Remember to include examples from the text about the characters, setting, and plot.

On a separate sheet of paper, use your prewriting plan to write a response paragraph, or make a new plan to write about your favorite book, short story, or play.

Argument Paragraph

An **argument paragraph** tries to convince readers to think or act in a certain way.

Parts of an Argument Paragraph

- An opening that presents the author's argument
- Reasons and details that provide evidence to support the argument
- Words and ideas that persuade the reader
- A conclusion that summarizes the argument

Opening
Presents the argument

Powerful Words
Persuade the reader

Evidence
Supports the argument

Conclusion
Summarizes the argument

The administration at Brooks Middle School should support the formation of a student-run newspaper. Under teacher guidance, we could plan, research, write, and publish articles about events and happenings that affect our school community. **First**, a newspaper would give us an opportunity to practice our research and writing skills. We would learn how to conduct interviews, gather data, clearly present ideas, and edit our work—all valuable skills that will help us in our classes. **Second**, a student newspaper is a fantastic way for us to communicate with each other. If someone wanted to form a new club or study group, then they would just have to put an announcement in the paper. **Finally**, a student paper will bring us together and help make us feel important and valuable. Other local middle schools that began student newspapers have had impressive results. Student writing scores greatly improved, and the students report a stronger sense of pride in their school. They feel they now have more of a voice and a greater sense of community. Aren't these all things that we want here as well? A student newspaper will teach valuable skills, share information, and improve school spirit. It's time the students at Brooks had a voice. After all, it is OUR school.

Other Transitions
In addition
Last
Therefore
Also
To begin with
To start
Next

Name _____

Follow your teacher's directions to complete this page.

We Do
1   We believe _____

_____. It is important because _____

_____

_____

_____

_____. To start, _____

_____

_____

_____

In addition, _____

_____

_____

_____

_____

In conclusion, _____

_____

_____

_____

You Do
2   On a separate sheet of paper, write an argument paragraph
about something you would like to change at your school.

You Do
3   On a separate sheet of paper, use your prewriting plan to write
an argument paragraph, or make a new plan to write about
whether or not your school should have an athletics program.

Book Review

A **book review** is a composition that contains the writer's analysis and opinion of a book or selection.

Parts of a Book Review

- An opening sentence that states the main idea and the author's opinion
- An analysis of setting, character, and plot that supports the author's opinion
- A closing sentence that restates the main idea and the author's recommendation

Opening Sentence
Gives main idea and author's opinion

Analysis
Presents story details that support author's opinion

Closing Sentence
Restates main idea and gives author's recommendation

My favorite part of *Science Friction* was the character development. The main character, Amanda, considers herself a "science geek," and she is not pleased about being grouped with "Ms. Perfect," the class clown, and "Mr. Silent" for their class project. We see her detached, organized personality when she uses scientific references to explain things, such as comparing the team members to "inert gases" that don't easily combine. **In addition**, the first-person point of view helps readers really understand what Amanda thinks about her non-science teammates.

The best part, however, is how Amanda changes in the story. Even though she isn't happy with her group, she still tries to work with them and compromises when they have different ideas. **In the end**, she discovers that she might have misjudged her teammates a bit and that she could learn some things from them. The "elements" that were reluctant to work together, she learns, end up producing a great science project.

This story has a realistic main character who learns a valuable lesson. I would recommend it to anyone who likes a good story.

Other Transitions
First
Later
Eventually
After
Next
Following

Name _____

Follow your teacher's directions to complete this page.

1 (We Do)   One of my favorite books is _____.

It is about _____

_____.

The main character _____

_____

_____

One important element of the story is _____

_____

_____

_____

Also, _____

_____

_____

In the end, _____

_____

_____

I would recommend this book to _____

_____

_____

2 (You Do)   On a separate sheet of paper, write a book review about your favorite novel.

3 (You Do)   On a separate sheet of paper, use your prewriting plan to write a book review, or make a new plan and write a review of a different book.

Argument: Prewriting

An **argument** seeks to convince readers to agree with the author's position.

Parts of an Argument

- An introduction that states the topic and the author's personal beliefs about the topic
- A body that uses logical reasoning and factual evidence to support the argument
- A conclusion that sums up the argument

East High School—first city high school, built 1890s

Crown Theater—only theater building left from 1920s

Valuable historical buildings in our town that should be preserved

County courthouse—first "modern" building, only limestone block left

Name _____

Follow your teacher's directions to complete this page.

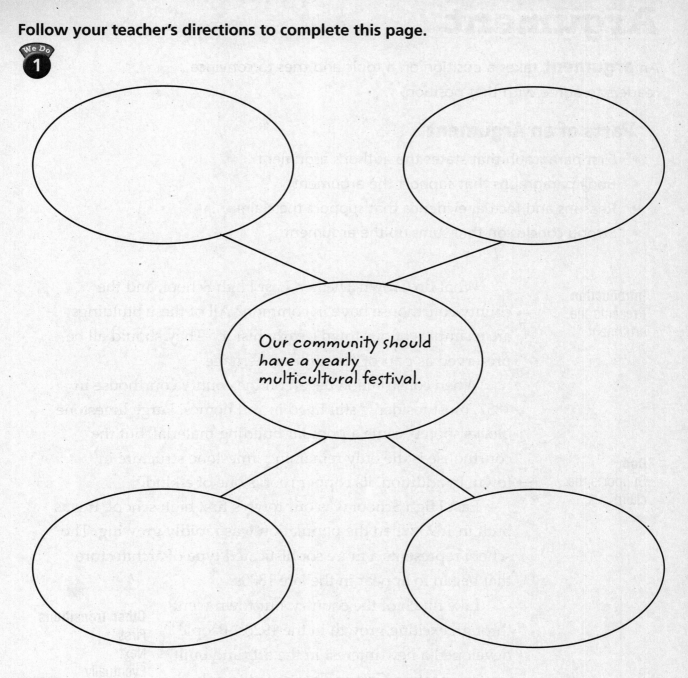

 1

Our community should have a yearly multicultural festival.

2 On a separate sheet of paper, complete a web for an argument about the importance of history museums.

3 On a separate sheet of paper, complete a web for an argument about why you should learn a second language.

Argument

An **argument** takes a position on a topic and tries to convince readers to agree with that position.

Parts of an Argument

- First paragraph that states the author's argument
- Body paragraphs that support the argument
- Reasons and factual evidence that support the claim
- Strong conclusion that sums up the argument

Introduction
Presents the argument

What do Crown Theater, East High School, and the county courthouse have in common? All of these buildings are examples of our town's early history. They should all be preserved as part of our cultural heritage.

Body
Supports the claim

When construction began on the county courthouse in 1857, most residents still lived in sod homes. Large limestone blocks soon became a popular building material, but the courthouse is the only remaining limestone structure in town. In addition, its copper roof is one of a kind.

East High School was our town's first high school. It was built in 1893 when the population was rapidly growing. The school represents a more sophisticated type of architecture that began to appear in the late 1800s.

Like much of the country, our town went through exciting growth in the 1920s. People developed a new interest in the arts and built several theaters. Crown Theater is the only building left from that time. People once flocked to its doors for an evening of entertainment. With new chairs and a paint job, it could probably open up for use again.

Other Transitions
First
Next
Eventually
Also
To begin with
Therefore
Last

Conclusion
Sums up the argument

These buildings all represent unique parts of our history, a history that is quickly disappearing. They are valuable for their architecture and historical significance. We should protect them while we still can.

Name _____

Follow your teacher's directions to complete this page.

We Do
1
_____

_____

_____.

First, _____

_____

_____

_____.

Additionally, _____

_____

_____. Also, _____

_____

_____.

Finally, _____

_____

_____.

In conclusion _____

_____

_____

_____

You Do
2 On a separate sheet of paper, write an argument about the importance of history museums.

You Do
3 On a separate sheet of paper, use your prewriting plan to write an argument, or make a new plan for a different argument.

Procedural Essay

A **procedural essay** is a composition that provides a step-by-step process to explain how something is done.

Parts of a Procedural Essay

- An opening that introduces the topic
- Transitions (first, next, last) that present steps in a clear order
- Relevant facts that prove statements are true
- A concluding statement that wraps up the main ideas

Introduction
Identifies topic

Transitions
Steps presented in order

Supporting Facts
Prove statements are true

Camping can be a fun and enjoyable way for families to relax and spend time together, but there are several steps you should take before setting off on your adventure. **First**, spend time researching possible campsites. Decide what you want to do, and **then** look for campgrounds that offer those activities. If you enjoy hiking and fishing, search for sites near trails and water.

Second, find and check all of your equipment. Gather everything you will need—cooking utensils, rain gear, sleeping bags—and check to make sure it all works. Set up your tent in the backyard beforehand to make sure there are no holes or tears and that you have all the pieces.

Third, plan your meals. Cooking over a campfire or camp stove is very different from cooking at home. Plan meals that are easy to make as well as nutritious and yummy.

Other Transitions
To begin
Later
Eventually
After
Next
Following

Fourth, always check the weather before setting out. A campout can easily be ruined by a steady rain or a surprise snow storm. If you are camping in the mountains, you should still be prepared for unexpected weather conditions.

Finally, relax and have fun. You are there to get away from the constant busyness of home, so roast those marshmallows, lay back, and enjoy the stars.

Concluding Statement

Name _____

Follow your teacher's directions to complete this page.

1 Have you ever wanted to _____?

The first thing to do is _____

_____

_____.

You also need to _____

_____

_____.

Next, make sure to _____

_____

_____

_____

_____.

Finally, _____

_____

_____

_____

_____.

2 On a separate sheet of paper, write a procedural essay about an activity that you enjoy.

3 On a separate sheet of paper, use your prewriting plan to write a procedural essay, or make a new plan that explains a different procedure.

Classification Essay

A **classification essay** explains a topic by discussing its parts.

Parts of a Classification Essay

- An introduction that presents the topic
- A brief summary that names the parts of the topic
- An explanation of each part
- A conclusion that wraps up and restates the main points

Introduction
Presents the topic

Brief Summary
Names the main parts of the topic

Body Paragraphs
Explain each part

Conclusion
Wraps up the main ideas and facts

Reptiles are a large group of animals that have been around for millions of years. They are vertebrates, have scaly skin, and usually lay eggs. They **also** are cold-blooded. There are four groups of reptiles alive today: snakes and lizards, turtles and tortoises, crocodilians, and the tuatara.

Snakes and lizards make up the largest group of reptiles with over 5,700 different species. Some lizards and all snakes are legless. Legless lizards are different from snakes in that lizards have eardrums and eyelids and snakes do not.

Turtles and tortoises are the **second** largest group of reptiles with over 200 species. They have shells protecting their bodies. Most of the shells are hard, but some are soft and leathery.

Crocodiles, alligators, caimans, and gavials are the **next** group, called crocodilians. There are 23 species, and they are the oldest and most advanced reptiles. They are more closely related to birds than to other reptiles.

The smallest group is the tuatara, which look like lizards. Tuatara live in New Zealand even though their closest relatives went extinct millions of years ago.

Reptiles may not be cute and cuddly, but they are an interesting and diverse group of animals that have been around for a long time.

Other Transitions
First
Later
Eventually
After
Following
Then
For example
Finally

Name _____

Follow your teacher's directions to complete this page.

1 _____ are _____

_____

_____

_____

_____. The first _____

_____

The second _____

_____

_____

_____

The next _____

_____

_____

_____. In addition _____

_____

_____

In conclusion, _____

_____

_____

2 On a separate sheet of paper, write a classification essay about your favorite activity or hobby.

3 On a separate sheet of paper, use your prewriting plan to write a classification essay, or make a new plan that explores a different topic.

Definition Essay

A **definition essay** explains the meaning of a word or phrase.

Parts of a Definition Essay

- An introduction that defines the word or phrase
- Examples and details that support and explain the definition
- Details that tell what the word means to the writer
- A summary that wraps up the definition and examples

Introduction
Defines the word

The dictionary defines "courage" as the ability to face danger or difficulty, but I think there is a lot more to it than that. Real courage requires an inner strength that most people don't know they have until they have to use it. I'm lucky because four of the most courageous people I know are in my own family.

Examples and Details
Support the definition

I'll **start** with my great-grandparents who lived in Atlanta, Georgia, during the 1960s. They sacrificed their livelihoods and many friendships when they joined the civil rights movement. They showed great courage by speaking out for what they knew was right even though their opinion was unpopular at the time.

My **next** example is my aunt, who shows courage when she runs into burning buildings to rescue people from fires. She has been a firefighter for ten years and says, "It's just part of the job." But I know she is very courageous. Not many people would risk their own lives to save the lives of complete strangers.

Transitions
First
To begin with
Later
Eventually
After
Following
Then
For example
Such as

Details
Tell what the word means to the writer

Finally, my little brother is the very definition of courage. He was born with a disease that will keep him in a wheelchair his entire life. He has faced five surgeries, will never know what it is like to kick a soccer ball, and yet always has a smile on his face and a kind word for everyone he meets.

Summary
Wraps up the definition and examples

These are the people I think of when I think of courage. They are brave, principled, and hopeful. They are my heroes.

Name _____

Follow your teacher's directions to complete this page.

1 The dictionary defines _____ as

_____. To

many people it means _____

_____. When I think

of _____

_____

_____

_____.

That is because _____

_____

_____.

In addition, _____

_____

_____.

That is why _____

_____

_____.

2 On a separate sheet of paper, write a definition essay about a word that is meaningful to you.

3 On a separate sheet of paper, use your prewriting plan to write a definition essay, or make a new plan about a different word.

Informational Essay: Prewriting

An **informational essay** uses facts and details to tell readers about a topic.

Parts of an Informational Essay

- An introduction that presents a clearly defined topic
- A body that gives main ideas with supporting details
- A conclusion that summarizes the ideas presented

Topic: Incan Gods

Inti—sun god, was supreme. Nourished the earth and crops.

Virocacha—made people from clay. Made sun, moon and stars.

Incas believed in many different gods that were connected to their daily lives.

Illapa—weather god

Zaramama—goddess of grain and corn

Name _____

Follow your teacher's directions to complete this page.

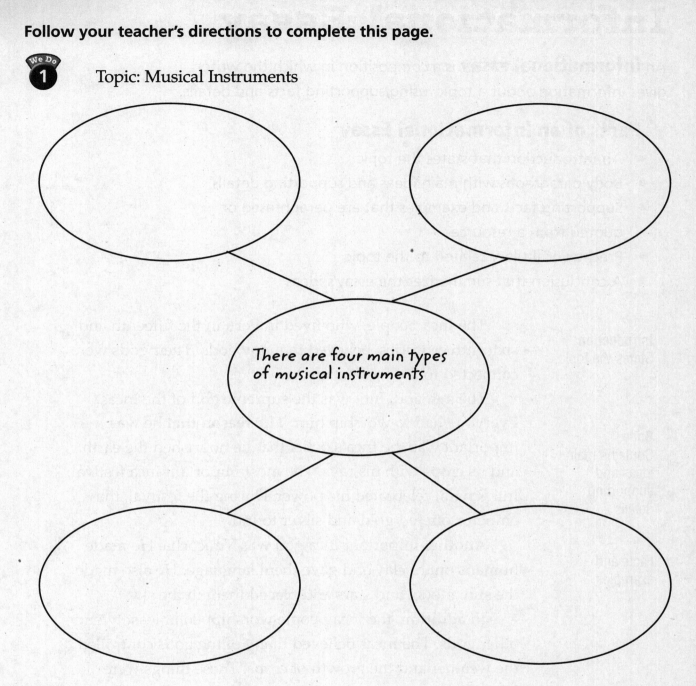

1 Topic: Musical Instruments

There are four main types of musical instruments

2 Research information about a Greek myth. On a separate sheet of paper, complete a web for an informational essay about the myth.

3 Research information about the belief system of Native Americans. On a separate sheet of paper, complete a web for an informational essay about Native American beliefs, or use what you have learned to improve a plan you have already made.

Informational Essay

An **informational essay** is a composition in which the writer gives information about a topic, using supporting facts and details.

✎ Parts of an Informational Essay

- An introduction that states the topic
- Body paragraphs with main ideas and supporting details
- Supporting facts and examples that are paraphrased or quoted from a resource
- Precise vocabulary related to the topic
- A conclusion that summarizes the essay's ideas

Introduction
States the topic

The Inca people, who lived in Peru in the fifteenth and sixteenth centuries, believed in many gods. Their gods were connected to the Inca's daily life.

The sun god, Inti, was the supreme god of the Incas. Everyone had to worship him. **The reason that** he was important was the Inca's belief that he nourished the earth

Body
Contains main ideas and supporting details

and its crops with his rays. The most important Inca festival, Inti Raymi, celebrated his power. During the festival, the emperor offered gold and silver to Inti.

Facts and examples

Another important Inca god was Viracocha. He made humans out of clay and gave them language. He also made the sun, moon, and stars and placed them in the sky.

In addition, the Inca people worshipped at least twenty other gods. The Incas believed many of the gods controlled the weather and the growth of crops. These things were very important to the Inca way of life. Zaramama, for example, was the goddess of grain and corn. Illapa was a weather god.

Conclusion
Summarizes ideas

In conclusion, the Incas worshipped many gods because they wanted to understand the world. By having gods that controlled different parts of their everyday world, they hoped that their worship would improve their lives.

Other Transitions
To begin with
Also
Second
Additionally
Finally
In summary
To sum up

Name _____

Follow your teacher's directions to complete this page.

1 _____

_____

_____

_____

(Main idea and details) _____

_____

_____

_____

(Main idea and details) _____

_____

_____

_____

In conclusion, _____

_____

_____

_____

2 On a separate sheet of paper, use your plan to write an informational essay about a Greek myth.

3 On a separate sheet of paper, use your prewriting plan to write an informational essay, or plan and write an informational essay about a topic of your choice.

Compare-Contrast Essay

A **compare-contrast essay** tells how two or more people, places, or things are alike and how they are different.

Parts of a Compare-Contrast Essay

- An introduction that tells the main idea
- A body that is organized logically: differences first, then similarities; similarities, then differences; or similarities and differences point by point
- Supporting details about similarities and differences
- A conclusion that sums up the essay

Introduction
Tells the topic of the essay

Body
Treats differences, then similarities

Supporting Sentences
Explain differences and similarities

Conclusion
Sums up the essay

Schools in America have changed a lot since the nineteenth century. Some things are still the same, though.

Schools in the early 1800s often contained all grades in just one room. Today, **however**, schools are usually bigger, and each grade has its own room. In the 1800s, supplies might have been limited to a slate, some chalk, and a few books. **In contrast**, classrooms today often have many supplies, from books to computers. Back then, the teacher was usually a woman, and she had to be unmarried. Now, **though**, teachers can be men or women, married or unmarried.

Even with all these differences, some things have remained pretty much the same. Today, people in the community are involved in their schools, **just as** they were back then. Parents still help out at the school, and students still help the rest of their town or city. **Also**, just as in the 1800s, the aim of schools today is to educate students.

If you traveled back in time to a nineteenth-century school, you probably would not recognize much. However, you would sure learn a lot!

Other Transitions
On the one hand
On the other hand
Unlike
Both
Also
Similarly

Name _____

Follow your teacher's directions to complete this page.

1 Traveling today is not the same as it was a hundred years ago, but certain things about it have not changed.

•_____

_____

However, _____

_____. In contrast, _____

_____

_____, though, _____

_____

_____

_____

_____ just as _____

_____. Also, _____

_____

_____

_____

_____

2 Think about the ways people used to send information one hundred years ago. Now think about how people do it today. On a separate sheet of paper, write a compare-contrast essay about how people communicated then and how they do now. Make sure to put your details in a logical order.

3 On a separate sheet of paper, use your prewriting plan to write a compare-contrast essay, or plan and write a new essay, comparing and contrasting the ways two cultures celebrate a holiday.

Problem-Solution Essay

A **problem-solution essay** is a composition that explains a problem and suggests possible solutions.

Parts of a Problem-Solution Essay

- An introduction with details and examples that make the problem clear to the reader
- Reasonable solutions that are each explained by details
- Transition words that link examples and signal each solution to the problem
- A conclusion that restates the author's position

Introduction
Explains the problem in detail

→ Community Park is a great place that offers activities for everyone, but an increase in traffic has made this jewel of our town dangerous to reach. There is no room for parking, so most people walk to Community Park from their homes or from parking lots several blocks away. Fast cars and dark streets make this walk risky, especially for families with young children. Fortunately, a few simple changes can help walkers stay safe.

Transition Words
Link examples and signal each solution

→ **To begin with**, lower the speed limit to 20 mph on the streets downtown. Slower-moving drivers can pay better attention to pedestrians and can stop faster. **In addition**, install stoplights at the crosswalks. This will discourage people from jaywalking in the middle of the street and force cars to stop for pedestrians.

Other Transitions
First, second, third
Then
After
Next
Following
First of all
For example

Details
Support reasonable solutions to the problem

→ **Finally**, add more street lamps. There are many evening events at Community Park, like summer concerts and baseball games, but there is little lighting after dark. Additional street lamps will not only make it easier for cars to see pedestrians but will make the park safer in general.

Conclusion
Restates the author's arguments

→ These measures will go a long way in making Community Park a fun and safe place for our entire community.

Name _____

Follow your teacher's directions to complete this page.

1 One problem that affects our class is _____

_____

_____

_____

We can solve this problem by _____

_____

First of all, _____

_____

For example, _____

_____

_____. In addition, _____

_____

_____

Last of all, _____

_____

_____

_____

2 On a separate sheet of paper, write a problem-solution essay about a problem at your school.

3 On a separate sheet of paper, use your prewriting plan to write a problem-solution essay, or make a new plan that solves a different problem.

Cause-Effect Essay

A **cause-effect essay** tells about something that happened and the person, object, or event that made it happen.

Parts of a Cause-Effect Essay

- A introduction that states a cause, an effect, or both
- Precise details that tell the causes, or why things happened
- Details that tell effects, or what happened
- Transition words or phrases that connect ideas
- A conclusion that describes the final effect

Topic Sentence
States an effect

Precise Details
Tell about the cause

More causes lead to effects

Conclusion
Tells the final effect

Other Transitions
As a result
After that
That's why
Since
So

More than three thousand years ago, a huge Greek army attacked the city of Troy on the shores of modern-day Turkey. This brought about the Trojan War, which went on for ten years. Both sides grew weary of the fighting, but neither could gain victory. **Finally,** Odysseus, one of the Greek leaders, devised a plan to end the war.

The Greeks built a large, wooden horse and, in the middle of the night, left it just outside the walls of Troy. **Then** they sailed their ships out of sight. **When** the Trojans awoke they saw no armies, only the wooden horse. They were convinced the Greeks had given up the war and left. The horse, they decided, was a gift from the defeated Greeks. Dragging the giant "gift" inside the city, the Trojans began to celebrate their victory.

Unknown to the Trojans, Odysseus and a handful of Greek soldiers waited, hidden inside the wooden horse. That night, the Greek army made its way back to Troy. When the Trojans finally fell asleep, Odysseus and his soldiers slipped out of the horse. They opened the gates of Troy, allowing the Greek army to pour into the city. Soon, Troy was destroyed. Odysseus's trick had brought the Greeks the victory.

Name _____

Follow your teacher's directions to complete this page.

1 Hurricane Katrina slammed into New Orleans in August of 2005.

_____

_____. Then _____

_____

_____. However, _____

_____

_____. While _____

_____

_____. Because of _____

_____

_____

_____

_____

_____

_____

_____

_____

_____

2 On a separate sheet of paper, plan and write a cause-effect essay about a historical event you learned about in school.

3 On a separate sheet of paper, use your prewriting plan to write a cause-effect paragraph, or plan and write a paragraph describing the causes and effects of a historical event.

Research Report: Prewriting

A **research report** uses facts taken from multiple sources to closely analyze an idea or topic.

Parts of a Research Report

- A thesis statement that introduces a clear topic
- A body with main ideas and supporting details
- Facts and examples gathered from research
- A conclusion that summarizes the ideas presented

Topic: Blue Whales

I. Background
  A. largest mammal
    1. 80-100 ft
    2. 100-200 tons
  B. found in every ocean
  C. eat krill

II. Endangered Species
  A. overhunted
    1. hundreds of thousands before 1900
    2. one whale provided 120 barrels of oil
    3. 29,000 killed in 1931
    4. nearly extinct by 1960s
  B. efforts to save whales
    1. hunting banned in 1966
    2. 1970 listed as endangered

III. Conclusion
  A. only between 5,000 and 12,000 remain
  B. conservation efforts can hopefully save them

Name _____

Follow your teacher's directions to complete this page.

1 **Topic:** Manatee

> I. Description
>
>   A.
>
>   B.
>
>   C.
>
> II. Habitat and Diet
>
>   A.
>
>   1.
>
>   2.
>
>   3.
>
>   B.
>
>   1.
>
>   2.
>
>   3.
>
> III. Conclusion
>
>   A.
>
>   B.

2 Choose an endangered insect. Research information about the insect's habitat, appearance, and why it is endangered. On a separate sheet of paper, complete an outline for a research paper about your chosen insect.

3 On a separate sheet of paper, complete an outline for an endangered species that interests you, or use what you have learned to improve a plan you have already made.

Research Report

A **research report** is a composition in which the writer closely examines a topic or idea. A research report uses factual information gathered and paraphrased from several sources.

Parts of a Research Report

- An introduction or thesis statement stating the topic
- Body paragraphs with main ideas and supporting details
- Facts and examples as supporting details
- A conclusion that sums up the main points

Introduction
Clearly states the topic

Body Paragraphs
Use details to support each main idea

Facts and Examples
Support the main ideas

Information Source
Tells where paraphrased information was found

Conclusion
Sums up the report

Introduction

The blue whale is thought to be the largest mammal on Earth. It may not hold that title for long. **It is endangered and may soon disappear.**

Blue whales are about 80 to 100 feet long and weigh from 100 to 200 tons. They are found in every ocean on Earth, and they eat mostly krill, which are tiny animals like shrimp (Hale 25). They are not a threat to humans, but humans are a terrible threat to them.

Endangered Species

Before the 1900s, there were hundreds of thousands of blue whales in the world's oceans. **However**, they were prized by whale hunters because of their great size. A single blue whale could provide up to 120 barrels of oil. In one year, 1931, over 29,000 whales were killed. By the 1960s, the blue whale was nearly extinct (Richards 100–101).

In 1966, the International Whaling Commission banned hunting of blue whales. **Soon after**, in 1970, the United States Fish and Wildlife Service listed the blue whale as endangered.

Although many of the blue whales are gone forever, there are still a few thousand left (Jenkins 90). With efforts by wildlife conservation groups, it is possible that these enormous creatures will be saved.

Other Transitions
To begin with
Meanwhile
Until
But
For instance
In conclusion

Follow your teacher's directions to complete this page.

We Do
1

Manatees are fascinating animals. They are also rare: they are an endangered species and only a few thousand remain.

(Heading) _____

(Main idea and details) _____

_____

_____

_____

_____

(Main idea and details) _____

_____

_____

_____

_____

_____

In conclusion, _____

_____

_____

You Do
2

Use your plan to write a research report about an endangered insect on a separate sheet of paper.

You Do
3

On a separate sheet of paper, use your prewriting plan to write a research report, or plan and write a research report about an endangered animal of your choice.

Opinion Essay

An **opinion essay** is a composition that presents the writer's view on a topic and provides support for that view.

Parts of an Opinion Essay

- An introduction that expresses the writer's opinion
- Brief summary and details that support the opinion
- The writer's own personal experience when it is relevant
- Reasons that are presented in logical order
- A summary that includes a recommendation

Introduction
States the writer's opinion

Details
Support the opinion

Reasons
In order of importance

Conclusion
Summary and recommendation

In "All Alone in the Universe," Maureen should have been more understanding and considerate of Debbie's feelings. **In the first place**, Maureen and Debbie had been best friends for a long time, so Maureen should have expected Debbie to be at least a little jealous of her friendship with Glenna. Who wouldn't have a hard time seeing her best friend become buddy-buddy with someone else?

Second, as Debbie's best friend, Maureen should have picked up on clues that Debbie was upset long before the abruptly-ended car ride. It is hard to believe that she didn't notice Debbie's grumpiness at the carnival or the tension. Having been abandoned by a best friend myself, I know how miserable Debbie was and that feeling is difficult to hide.

Finally, Maureen could have done more to help Debbie and Glenna get along, instead of letting them compete for her attention. If I were Debbie, I might think about looking for a new best friend.

All in all, I wouldn't hesitate to recommend "All Alone in the Universe." I was able to relate to everything that happened, and I suspect most readers would feel the same.

Other Transitions
First
Later
Eventually
After
Next
Following
Then
For example

Name _____

Follow your teacher's directions to complete this page.

We Do
1   I think it is important to _____

_____. One reason it is important is _____

_____

_____

_____

Another reason _____

_____

_____

_____

For example, _____

_____

_____

_____

_____

In conclusion _____

_____

_____

_____

_____

You Do
2   On a separate sheet of paper, write an opinion essay about an issue that bothers you.

You Do
3   On a separate sheet of paper, use your prewriting plan to write an opinion essay, or make a new plan that explores a different topic.

Problem-Solution Essay

A **problem-solution essay** states a problem and suggests at least one solution.

Parts of a Problem-Solution Essay

- A topic sentence that states the problem
- Details and examples that make the problem clear
- One or more reasonable solutions, with details that explain them
- Transition words that link examples and signal solutions
- A concluding statement that sums up the writer's opinion

Topic Sentence
States the problem

Examples
Make the problem clear

Possible Solutions

Details
Explain solutions

Concluding Statement
Sums up the writer's opinion

Our community has a lot of dog lovers, but there is no place for them to take their pets without bothering the people who don't like dogs. I have two ideas to fix this problem.

Our local park is a beautiful place, but dog owners don't always pick up after their pets. **In addition**, owners often let their dogs off the leash, and this bothers and even scares other people. I can offer two possible ways to solve the problem. The **first** is to enforce the dog laws. There are already signs about keeping dogs on a leash and picking up after them. Ticketing people who don't obey those rules would help. My **second** idea is to create a dogs-only area. There is a section of the park that is rarely used. With a fence, it could work really well as a meeting place for dogs and their owners. It would be a place where pets could run and play off-leash.

In conclusion, while some people might object to helping dogs, dogs are very important to many people, and dogs certainly deserve a place to have fun.

Other Transitions
To begin with
Also
Not only
In closing
Therefore

Name _____

Follow your teacher's directions to complete this page.

1   A lot of kids in our community want to skateboard and inline skate,

but there really isn't any place to do either activity. _____

_____

_____. In addition, _____

_____

_____. First, _____

_____

_____

_____.

Second, _____

_____

_____

_____

_____

_____.

In conclusion, _____

_____

2   On a separate sheet of paper, plan and write a problem-solution
essay about a problem in your school. Include at least one
possible solution.

3   On a separate sheet of paper, use your prewriting plan to write
a problem-solution essay, or plan and write an essay about a
problem in your community and a possible solution.

Persuasive Letter

In a **persuasive letter,** the writer tries to persuade the reader to think or do something.

Parts of a Persuasive Letter

- Often, business letter format: heading, inside address, greeting, body, closing, and signature
- A goal, or opinion, with a specific action for the reader to take
- Reasons that support the writer's goal
- Language that is more formal than in a friendly letter

462 Lantern Ln.
Coral Springs, FL 33065
April 23, 2012

The Sun Chronicle
1007 West St.
Coral Springs, FL 33065

Other Closings
Yours truly
Regards
Best
Sincerely yours
Respectfully

To the Editor:

Goal
Tells the action the writer wants the reader to take

 I am writing about your editorial stating that our city should have fewer police officers. I believe that you should rethink your position.

Reasons
Support the writer's goal

 First of all, you write that our low crime rate means we need fewer police officers. I think that our crime rate is low *because* of all our well-trained officers. **Further,** you say fewer police officers would cost our city less. According to our mayor, getting rid of officers would cause crime to rise and would cost our city more. **Finally,** if we fired some of our officers, they would have trouble finding jobs. At this time, we do not want more unemployed people in our city.

Formal language

 To sum up, I think you should reconsider. You could write a new editorial praising officers for their hard work!

Sincerely,

Marina Ellis

Name _____

Follow your teacher's directions to complete this page.

1

                                  _____

                                    _____

                                    _____

_____

_____

_____

To _____ :

_____

_____

_____

_____

_____

_____

_____

_____

                               Yours truly,

                               _____

2 On a separate sheet of paper, plan and write a persuasive letter to the school board persuading them not to lengthen the school year.

3 On a separate sheet of paper, use your prewriting plan to write a persuasive letter, or plan and write a letter to the editor of your local paper. Write to agree or disagree with a recent editorial. Try to persuade readers to take action.

Argument: Prewriting

An **argument** makes a claim and tries to convince readers to agree with that claim.

Parts of an Argument

- An introduction that states the author's claim or position
- A body that supports the claim with reasons and evidence, such as facts and examples
- Clear connections between the writer's claim and the reasons and evidence that support it
- Conclusion that sums up the argument

Topic: More Technology is Needed in Schools

is a basic skill	needed for jobs	good for the country
technology is everywhere need it to function hard to go a day without it	almost all jobs require some tech skills can't get work without computer knowledge more tech knowledge means a better job	keeps us competitive might keep tech companies here

Name _____

Follow your teacher's directions to complete this page.

 1 **Topic: We shouldn't rely too much on technology**

 2 **Topic:**

3 On a separate sheet of paper, use your prewriting plan to write
an argument, or make a new plan for a different argument.

Argument

An **argument** is an essay that tries to persuade readers to agree with the author's position.

Parts of an Argument

- Introduction that states the author's claim or position
- Body paragraphs that support the claim with reasons and evidence
- Conclusion that sums up the argument

Introduction
States the claim

We live in a world where technology is advancing faster than it ever has before. Unfortunately, many students still have very little experience with technology at school. It is important that students have access to technology in school and learn how to use it.

To begin with, technology is everywhere in our country. From doing research on the Internet to talking on a cell phone, it is almost impossible to spend a day not interacting with technology. Just like reading and math, understanding technology is now a basic skill required to function in society.

Facts and Reasoning
Support the claim

In addition, technology is also an important job skill. Not everyone needs to know how to build robots or design solar panels, but nearly every job requires at least some computer use. Students without basic computer knowledge will have trouble finding a job.

Other Transitions
To start
Next
Eventually
First
Therefore
Last
For example

Finally, technology education is ultimately good for our country. Most major technology companies are in other countries. If we don't start teaching kids now, we won't be able to compete.

Conclusion
Sums up the argument

Technology is a basic skill that should be taught in all of our schools. Without it, American students will be left in the chalk dust.

Name _____

Follow your teacher's directions to complete this page.

We Do 1   One important skill that every student must learn is _____

_____

_____

_____

First of all, _____

_____

_____

_____

Next, _____

_____

_____. For example _____

_____

_____

Most importantly, _____

_____

_____

Therefore, _____

_____

_____

You Do 2   On a separate sheet of paper, write an argument about the use of cell phones in your school.

You Do 3   On a separate sheet of paper, use your prewriting plan to write an argument, or make a new plan for a different argument.

Narrative Poem

A **narrative poem** tells a story. Sound techniques, such as rhythm, rhyme, and repetition, make it enjoyable to listen to. Narrative poetry comes in several forms, such as ballads and epics.

Parts of a Narrative Poem

- An opening that sets the scene for the rest of the poem
- A body that develops characters, setting, and plot
- Meter—a pattern of rhythm, or stressed and unstressed syllables
- A rhyme scheme, or pattern of rhyming words
- Repetition of words, lines, or even whole stanzas

Opening
First stanza sets the scene.

The <u>cries</u> came <u>late</u> one <u>summer</u> <u>night</u>:
Loud <u>howling</u> <u>shrieks</u> and <u>lots</u>
Of <u>crashing</u>, <u>just</u> like <u>cymbals</u> <u>or</u>
A <u>tumbling</u> <u>rack</u> of <u>pots</u>.

"<u>Mom</u>!" yelled <u>Claude</u>, "I <u>hate</u> to <u>say</u>,

Rhyme Scheme
The second and fourth line of each stanza rhyme.

A <u>tiger's</u> <u>in</u> the <u>field</u>.
And <u>did</u> you <u>hear</u> that <u>metal</u> <u>clang</u>?
It's <u>got</u> a **sword** and **shield**."

"A <u>tiger</u>, <u>here</u> in <u>Little</u> <u>Rock</u>?
I <u>don't</u> think <u>I</u> <u>accept</u> that.
And <u>one</u> who <u>wields</u> a **sword** and **shield**?
That <u>must</u> be <u>one</u> <u>adept</u> cat!"

Characters, setting, and plot

"Still, <u>let's</u> make <u>sure</u>," Mom <u>said</u>, and <u>so</u>
The <u>two</u> sleuths <u>checked</u> the <u>scene</u>.
They <u>shuffled</u> <u>through</u> the <u>fog</u> and <u>dark</u>,
Right <u>past</u> Claude's <u>trampoline</u>.

Meter
The stress is on every other syllable.

And <u>what</u> they <u>found</u> will <u>chill</u> your <u>blood</u>!
For <u>there</u>, beneath the <u>moon</u>:
The **sword** and **shield** were <u>garbage</u> <u>cans</u>–
The <u>tiger</u>, <u>a</u> rac<u>coon</u>!

Narrative Poetic Devices
repetition
onomatopoeia
alliteration
assonance
imagery

Name _____

Follow your teacher's directions to complete this page.

1 Before her eyes, Irene beheld
A terrifying sight.

_____

_____

_____

_____

_____

_____

_____

_____

_____

_____

_____

_____

_____

_____

_____

2 On a separate sheet of paper, plan and write a narrative poem about a person facing a physical challenge, such as climbing a steep mountain. Use regular rhyme and meter to make your poem fun to listen to.

3 On a separate sheet of paper, plan and write a narrative poem about someone coming home from a long journey or a topic of your choice.

Field Notes

Field notes are observations made "in the field" at a particular location—a park, a school, a library, or even a store or market.

Parts of Field Notes

- A record of sights, sounds, events, impressions, feelings, and questions
- An organization by category: Setting, Observations, Reflections
- Figurative language, such as similes, metaphors, and personification, to vividly express ideas

Setting
The *what, when, where, how long*

Observations
The events and the writer's impressions

Figurative Language
The words that vividly express the observations

Reflections
A summary of what the writer saw and heard

Setting: It is 9:30 on a Saturday morning and I'm watching my sister Petra's karate class. It's been thirty minutes, and the class is almost over. There are twelve students ranging in age from 7–12, one teacher, and an assistant. Most of the floor is covered with thick foam mats. Fifteen observers sit on a cold, hard, metal bench along one wall facing a row of mirrors on the other wall.

Observations: Petra is positioned in the middle of the front row. She is the youngest and smallest student, but she has the best concentration. Her eyes focus like a cat waiting to pounce, and her stance is strong as steel. Balancing on her right leg, she doesn't move. She is a statue—unwavering, unchanging. The student next to her splats on the floor like a bug on a windshield, but Petra doesn't flinch. The sensei calls out numbers, and Petra performs the moves flawlessly. Downward block, front punch, rising block, "Ki-Yi!" Reflected in the mirror is seemingly effortless coordination, steady and graceful as a dancer.

Reflections: Karate isn't really about fighting but concentration and discipline. To succeed, you have to be able to tune out everything going on around you and focus on your current task. I wonder if Petra will always have such dedication.

Other Figurative Phrases
leaves dance in the wind
quiet as a falling feather
he is a turbulent ocean

Name _____

Follow your teacher's directions to complete this page.

1 **Setting** It is _____ o'clock on a _____. I
am in _____

_____. _____ minutes

have passed. _____

_____.

Observations I see _____

_____

_____.

It sounds like _____

_____

_____. The _____ feels _____

_____

_____

_____.

Reflections Based on my observations, I know that _____.

_____

_____

_____

2 On a separate sheet of paper, write field notes for a location at
your school.

3 On a separate sheet of paper, use your prewriting plan to write
field notes.

Radio Script

A **radio script** seeks to convince listeners to buy a product.

✏ Parts of a Radio Script

- A clear goal
- Reasons to buy the product
- A memorable take-away, or lasting impression
- May have an announcer, sound effects, voice-over, and characters
- Formal or informal voice as appropriate for subject and audience

Sound Effects
Set the scene

Announcer
Gives detailed information about the product

Informal Voice
Appeals to young audience

Take-away
Leaves listener with a lasting idea or impression

Sound Effect: [*General **noise and commotion** at a theme park, runs through entire script and includes sound effects below; becomes softer when narrator or characters are speaking.*]

Narrator: Come one, come all to the New Century Water and Fun Park! We've got something for everyone, including mini-rides for the kiddos.

Sound Effect: [*Children **laughing***]

Child 1:   Mommy, I want to go again!

Narrator: Water rides for the family.

Sound Effect: [***Whoosh and splash***]

Child 2:   [*giggling*] Look, Daddy's all wet!

Narrator: Roller coasters and terrifying thrill rides for all you daredevils out there!

Sound Effect: [***Roller coaster with screams***]

Teen 1:   Man! That was totally awesome!

Teen 2:   Dude, you should have seen your face!

Narrator: That's right! New Century is THE place to be for cool rides and hot deals for the entire family. So if you're looking for an unforgettable adventure that everyone will enjoy, then come on down to New Century! Visit our website for special discount offers.

Other Sound Effects
Footsteps
Dog barking
Car engine
Door slamming
Music
Typing
Siren

Name _____

Follow your teacher's directions to complete this page.

1 Sound Effect: _____

Announcer: _____

_____

Sound Effect: _____

_____

_____

_____

_____

Announcer: _____

_____

_____

_____

_____

_____

Sound Effect: _____

_____

Announcer: _____

_____

2 On a separate sheet of paper, write a radio script for a product that you use.

3 On a separate sheet of paper, use your prewriting plan to write a radio script, or make a new plan for a different product.

Personal Narrative: Prewriting

A **personal narrative** is a true story about the writer's life.

Parts of a Personal Narrative

- A beginning that catches the reader's attention
- A middle that explains the events in sequential (time) order
- An ending that wraps up events and tells how the writer felt
- Events told in the first-person point of view
- Vivid words that show the writer's personality

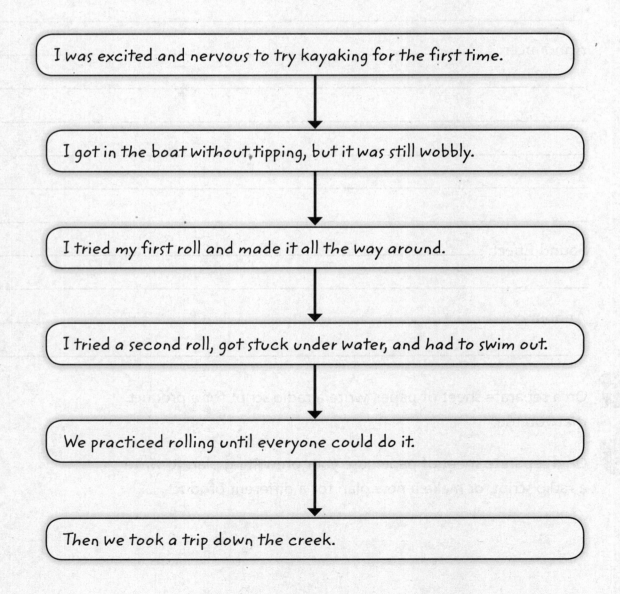

I was excited and nervous to try kayaking for the first time.

↓

I got in the boat without tipping, but it was still wobbly.

↓

I tried my first roll and made it all the way around.

↓

I tried a second roll, got stuck under water, and had to swim out.

↓

We practiced rolling until everyone could do it.

↓

Then we took a trip down the creek.

Name _____

Follow your teacher's directions to complete this page.

 1 Topic: _____.

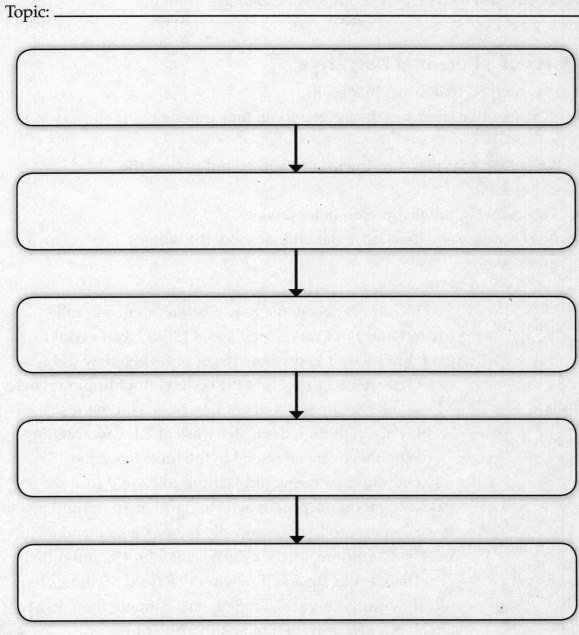

 2 On a separate sheet of paper, complete a flow chart about visiting a place for the first time.

 3 On a separate sheet of paper, complete a flow chart about trying a strange food for the first time, or use what you have learned to improve a chart you have already made.

Personal Narrative

A **personal narrative** tells about a real experience from the writer's life.

Parts of a Personal Narrative

- A beginning that draws readers in
- A middle that describes the experience in time order, or sequence
- An ending that tells how the events worked out or how the writer felt
- Events told in the first-person point of view
- Precise words and descriptive details that show the writer's personality

Beginning
Description that draws readers in

Middle
Describes events in time order

Details that show what the writer is like

Ending
Wraps up the narrative and tells how the writer felt

I had never been in a kayak before, so I was really excited to try it. I was scared, too. I knew kayaks could roll over, but I didn't know how to get out when they did.

First we had to get into the boat without tipping it over. My kayak had a pretty flat bottom, but it still felt really wobbly. Even though the water was cold, I was sweating!

When we were all seated in the little boats, the instructor told us we would learn to roll. We'd turn the kayaks over on purpose! Then we'd roll them upright again. If we couldn't roll, we would slip out of the seat and swim the kayak to shore. I took a deep, shaky breath and rolled.

There I was, upside down in my kayak! My lungs felt like they would burst. I'd rolled hard enough, though. My kayak popped upright. I felt really proud to have done it right -- until my second try! That time I got stuck upside down underwater. I got water up my nose, and I had to swim out. We rolled the kayaks over and over. **Finally,** everyone could do it, and we were ready to head down the creek. I couldn't believe I learned how to roll a kayak in just one day!

Other Transitions
When it started
After that
Next
Also
Soon
Before long
In the end

Name _____

Follow your teacher's directions to complete this page.

We Do 1

I was really excited about _____

_____. First, _____

_____

_____

_____. When _____

_____

_____

Later on, _____

_____

_____

What surprised me was _____

_____

_____

_____

_____

Finally, _____

_____

_____

You Do 2

On a separate sheet of paper, write a personal narrative about visiting a place for the first time.

You Do 3

On a separate sheet of paper, use your prewriting plan to write a personal narrative, or plan and write a personal narrative about trying a strange food for the first time.

Prewriting

Writing is easier if you break the process into five stages. The stages are prewriting, drafting, revising, editing, and publishing. As you write, you can go back to any stage. **Prewriting** is the planning stage before you start to write.

Prewriting

- First, pick a topic. Then write your ideas about the topic. Think about your purpose for writing, and ask yourself what your audience will need to know.
- Choose a topic or main idea for your work.
- You can use a graphic organizer to explore your topic or put your ideas in a logical order.

1 **Brainstorm a list.**

- Rock climbing
- We need a new track
- My sister, the biologist
- Uncle Pete comes home

2 **Gather information.**

Title: Uncle Pete's Return

Setting: Gabe's front porch	**Characters:** Gabe, his parents, Uncle Pete

Plot: Gabe sees a tall man get out of a taxi. He is bearded, dirty, exhausted, and dressed in a strange outfit.

Gabe realizes this stranger is Uncle Pete, who has been in the Himalayas.

Gabe shouts and races to hug Uncle Pete..

3 Organize the information.

Choose the graphic organizer that works best with your Task, Audience, and Purpose (TAP). Some graphic organizers can be used for different types of writing.

Idea-support Map

Main idea

Detail

Detail

Detail

Chart for How-to Paragraphs

How to _____	Tiltle
Materials:	Materials
Step 1	
Step 2	
Step 3	Steps
Step 4	
Step 5	

Persuasive Writing

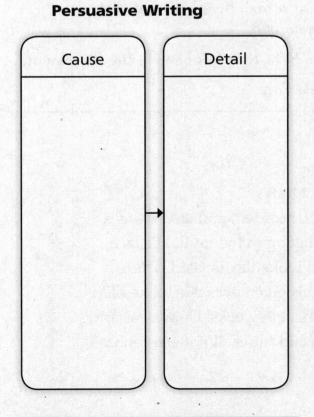

Cause	Detail

Sequence of Events Flow Chart for Informative or Narrative Writing

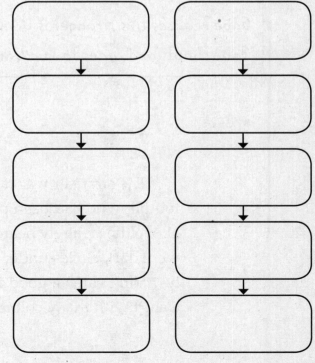

Drafting

Drafting is the second step of the writing process. When you draft, you use your prewriting plan to write what you planned.

Drafting

- Sometimes your plan or graphic organizer has all the information you need. Write your main ideas and details as complete sentences.
- At other times, you may need to expand your ideas further. For example, add vivid description and details to a narrative.
- Organize your writing logically. For example, group related ideas in a paragraph with a topic sentence.

Narrative

Title: Uncle Pete's Return

Setting: Gabe's front porch   **Characters:** Gabe, his parents, Uncle Pete

Plot: Gabe sees a tall man get out of a taxi. He is bearded, dirty, exhausted, and dressed in a strange outfit.

Gabe realizes this stranger is Uncle Pete, who has been in the Himalayas.

Gabe shouts and races to hug Uncle Pete.

Draft

The stranger was tall, bearded, and as dirty as a toddler who had been playing in the mud. His face above the scraggly beard looked exhausted. There were dark circles under his green eyes. He looked like he hadn't eaten a good meal in weeks. He was wearing a shirt with many colors and unusual patterns on it.

Persuasive

Topic: We need a new track.

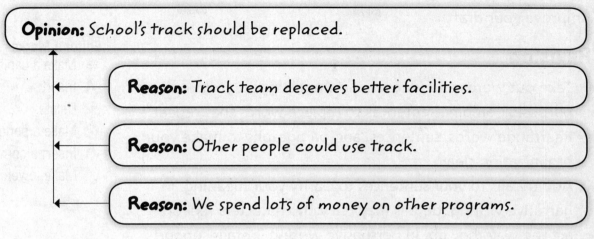

Opinion: School's track should be replaced.

Reason: Track team deserves better facilities.

Reason: Other people could use track.

Reason: We spend lots of money on other programs.

Draft

Our school needs to replace our crumbly, worn-out track right away. For one thing, our track team deserves a better place to practice. The team is very talented, but we have a hard time running on the old track. How will we have a chance at another league championship if we're always slipping on the starting line?

Revising

Revising is the third stage in the writing process. When you revise, you improve your draft.

Revising

- Take out words and ideas that do not support your topic or purpose. Combine sentences to replace words that repeat.
- Rearrange words, sentences, and paragraphs to make your organization clear.
- Add details to your sentences to clarify your meaning. In narrative writing, details may tell why characters feel or act the way they do. In persuasive writing, details support opinions.
- Use editing marks to show your changes.

Editor's Marks
≡ Make a capital.
∧ Insert.
ℛ Delete.
⊙ Make a period.
∧ Insert a comma.
/ Make lowercase.

Sample Revised Narrative

Draft

As the strange-looking man walked toward them, Gabe ∧ *and his parents*

stood up. *in alarm* ∧ ~~He scratched his chin with his left hand.~~ ~~His parents~~

~~stood up, too.~~ ~~Gabe and his parents~~ *They* realized that

there was something ~~unusual~~ *oddly familiar* ∧ about this man.

Gabe was afraid at first. Gabe ~~thought he~~ recognized

him.

Revising Tips:
- Add or change details.
- Move sentences for clarity.
- Combine sentences.
- Delete unnecessary details.

Other Ways to Revise

- Add transition words to make sentences and ideas flow more smoothly.
- Replace dull or vague words with more vivid and specific words.
- Add dialogue or quotations to make your narrative or essay more interesting.
- Rewrite unexciting sentences to show your voice and personality.

Sample Revised Persuasive Essay

Draft

Other ~~people~~ *students at our school and members of our community* could use the track, too. The soccer team could do their warm-ups on the track. ~~They do passing and~~ *Then they wouldn't have to run laps around the parking lot.* ~~shooting drills on the soccer field.~~ *and football* The baseball team*s* can use the track to practice running. ~~The football team can use the track to practice.~~ *Runners* ~~Other people~~ from the community can use the track to run when the sports teams aren't using it.

Editing

Editing, or proofreading, is the stage of the writing process that follows revising. During this stage, you look for and correct errors in your draft.

Editing

- Reread your writing.
- Check your punctuation, capitalization, and grammar. Use a dictionary, thesaurus, or grammar handbook if necessary.
- If you edit on paper, use editor's marks.
- If you edit on the computer, use the spelling and grammar checker. Then review your work. The computer does not catch everything.

> **Editor's Marks**
> ≡ Make a capital.
> ∧ Insert.
> ✗ Delete.
> ⊙ Add a period.
> ∧ Insert a comma.
> / Make lowercase.

Title: Uncle Pete's Return

Gabe's mouth dropped open. That's uncle Pete!" he shouted.
He jumped off the porch, He ran to him. Sure enough, under
the dirt and above the beerd, Uncle Petes green eyes twinkled.

Topic: The school needs a new track.

Finally, we spend lot's of money on other school programs.
The Football team just got new goalposts the marching band
has knew uniforms. Cleerly, are school has a big enough
budget for a new track!

Publishing

Publishing is the final step of the writing process. To publish your writing is to share it with your audience. There are many ways to publish your writing.

Publishing

- When you publish, you prepare a final version of your writing, either electronically or by hand, to present to an audience.
- Your final product can be a speech or other oral presentation, a poster or other visual presentation, or a printed item like a book or a report. It can also combine different forms of communication in a multimedia presentation. You might include drawings, charts, graphs, or photographs.

Story for an oral reading

> Use wide margins, and skip lines to make your piece easy to read.

Uncle Pete's Return

Gabe sat on the front porch with his parents. It was a
[Say this slowly.]
sweltering summer evening. The only sound in the still night

air was the crickets, sawing away like tiny violinists. Then Gabe

noticed a taxicab driving slowly down the street. To his
[Sound excited.]
shock, it stopped right in front of the house!

> Write notes that will help you use your voice in interesting ways.

Multimedia presentation slide

> Use an attention-grabbing title.

> Tell your audience what your main points will be.

We need a new track!

- Track team deserves better facilities.
- New track will be good for the community.
- School can afford it.

> Use clip art or photos to make your presentation fun to look at.

Evidence

Writing traits are the qualities found in all good writing. The six writing traits are evidence, organization, purpose, elaboration, development, and conventions. **Evidence** is the details, examples, and facts you include in informative and persuasive writing.

Evidence

- Do research to find facts, examples, and reasons. Take notes.
- Remove any ideas that do not relate to your topic.
- List facts and related details to see if your writing topic is a good one. If you can't come up with enough interesting facts, reasons, or details, choose another topic.
- Develop and reinforce your topic by adding more details facts, or reasons to inform or persuade.

Possible Topics:

-whales

-blue whales and orca whales

-food allergies

-benefits of gluten-free diet

I think there is too much information about this topic.

This idea is focused.

Now I know this is a strong topic because I can find just the right amount of information.

Topic: Blue Whales and Orca Whales

Facts:

-both are mammals

-blue whales have baleen and orca whales have teeth

-blue whales can eat up to 8,000 pounds of krill

-orca whales eat fish, squid, birds and other mammals

-both travel in pods

Informative Writing

- Organize details about a topic
- Possible graphic organizers for ideas: Venn diagram, note cards, sequence chart

Musical Instruments

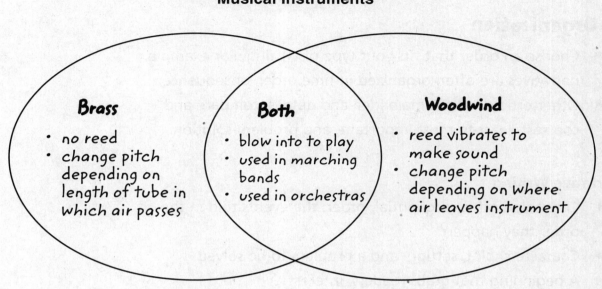

Brass
- no reed
- change pitch depending on length of tube in which air passes

Both
- blow into to play
- used in marching bands
- used in orchestras

Woodwind
- reed vibrates to make sound
- change pitch depending on where air leaves instrument

Persuasive Writing

- Think of reasons to support your goal or opinion
- Possible graphic organizers for ideas: idea-support map, column chart, main idea and details chart

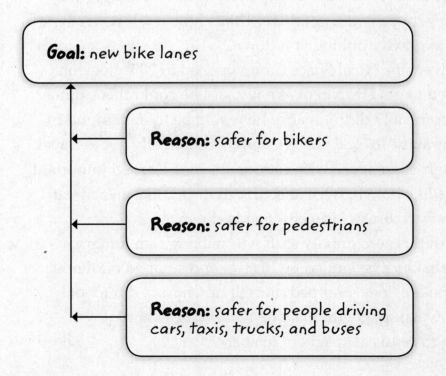

Goal: new bike lanes

Reason: safer for bikers

Reason: safer for pedestrians

Reason: safer for people driving cars, taxis, trucks, and buses

Organization

Organization is the order in which you present your ideas. Different types of writing require different kinds of organization.

Organization

- Choose an order that fits your type of writing. For example, narratives are often organized in time order, or sequence.
- Other orders include main idea and details, compare and contrast, least-to-most important, and problem-solution

Narrative Writing

- Chronological, or sequential, order: the events told in the order they happen
- Characters, plot, setting, and a problem to be solved
- A beginning that grabs readers' interest
- A middle with interesting details about the events
- An end that tells how the story worked out or how the writer felt

Beginning → Joey jumped up and down on the space shuttle's trampoline. It was a long way up and an even longer way down—if you could get there. That's how it felt when there was no gravity pulling you down.

Ever since Real Space Camp opened in 2051, Joey had wanted to go. His parents finally said he could this summer. They probably didn't realize he would be flying around in

Middle → zero gravity. In Real Space Camp, kids actually got to travel through outer space with astronauts. Joey learned important things like how to twist and turn in the air like an acrobat and how to brush his teeth upside-down.

All this zero gravity stuff was making him hungry, though. Once he landed on his feet and stepped off the

End → trampoline, Joey strapped himself down for a dinner of microwave spaghetti. Then he realized how hard it was going to be to eat spaghetti in space!

Informative Writing

- Information presented in a logical order
- An introduction that grabs readers' attention
- A body that presents information, explains ideas, or defines important terms
- A conclusion that summarizes the information

Introduction →

Hunter-gatherers were ancient people who hunted for animals and gathered plants for food. They used bows and arrows and spears to catch wild animals. They picked berries, wild grains, and fruit to eat.

Body →

Most of the hunter-gatherer societies were nomadic. This means they did not live in one place for too long. Many times, they had to move to find more food.

Conclusion →

Soon people began to farm instead of hunting and gathering. With farming, there was less threat of running out of food. It was a better and easier way to feed more people.

Persuasive Writing

- An introduction, body, and conclusion like informative writing
- Reasons presented in a logical order

Reasons →

There are many reasons why watching a lot of television is bad for you. First, looking at a television screen for a long time can strain your eyes. Reading a book uses your brain in a much better way and hurts your eyes a lot less. Second, television doesn't allow you to use your creativity. You could write a poem, draw a picture, or write a play of your own instead of just watching shows on TV. Finally, you could be playing sports or exercising to stay healthy. When you watch television, all you do is sit and stare. Try turning off the TV for an hour a day and see how your life changes!

Purpose

Good writers pay attention to the reason they are writing, or **purpose**. They clearly communicate the purpose in the opening and remind readers of it in the closing. They use descriptive, exciting words and a strong voice from the beginning to pull readers in. Your word choice can show your emotions, feelings, and personality.

Purpose

- Think about your task to identify the purpose. Are you writing to entertain, to inform, or to persuade?
- Keep your task, audience, and purpose in mind as you choose words. The words you choose set the tone of your writing. Tone is how the author feels about the subject and audience.
- Tone varies depending on the purpose. Persuasive writing can have a personal or impersonal tone. Informative writing is often more formal. Expressive writing can have many tones, such as friendly, warm, or humorous.
- Grab your readers' attention in the opening as you communicate your purpose. For informative writing, let your readers know your topic, and when writing persuasively, state your opinion. In narratives, describe the characters, setting, and situation.

The writer of this narrative begins by describing a character. Words like *sauntered* and *cascading* give details about the character.

The tone is clear from the beginning. The writer is in awe of the main character.

The writer is establishing the situation. The word choice does not say the character is confident, but tells us how the writer feels about the character.

She <u>sauntered</u> into the room, her long brown hair <u>flowing</u> behind her and <u>cascading</u> down onto her <u>brightly</u> <u>colored</u> shirt. Everyone in the room turned to look at her. She just had that kind of presence. Someone called her name on the other side of the room. <u>She could have looked toward that person, but she didn't need to.</u> She just kept walking, slowly and purposefully.

Elaboration

Precise **elaboration,** or the words and phrases a writer chooses, gives information and helps paint a clear picture for readers. It makes characters, settings, actions, and events more vivid. Replacing unclear words with words that are more exact makes for more interesting reading.

Elaboration

- Look at each word you use. See if it really describes the person, place, thing, or situation the way you want it to. If you can be more precise, revise.
- Think about your purpose for writing. See if you are including enough description and information. If not, add dialogue, facts, or vivid details.
- You can affect your readers' reaction by speaking directly to them, by using figurative language, and by repeating important words.
- Choose words and phrases to match your task, audience, and purpose.

Purpose: persuade readers to agree that reality TV is disgusting

I think reality TV has gone too far. Reality TV shows are garbage for the eyes. Garbage goes into these shows, and garbage comes out. Do we really need to waste our time watching people behave badly?

Purpose: entertain readers by describing how incredible my visit to Bruges was

As I wandered through the city of Bruges, Belgium, the Middle Ages came to life around me. The city was like a jewel, with sparkling canals, step-roofed brick houses, and peaceful gardens. I felt that I was wandering through a long-ago time.

Development

When writing narratives, good writers add vivid details and descriptions to **develop** believable characters, settings, and situations.

Development

- Describe characters and settings using concrete and figurative language. Words and phrases such as *with eyes as wide as saucers, majestic mountains,* and *as honest as Abe Lincoln* help readers visualize story elements.
- Develop and reinforce events and experiences that resolve conflicts in the story.
- Use transitions such as *this afternoon, last month, before sunrise,* and *after school* to move the plot along.
- Make your writing interesting by writing different kinds of sentences, varying how you begin sentences, and providing different sentence structures to create compound and complex sentences.

"Today's the day I give back to my community," Jacob thought <u>as he stretched his long limbs before leaping out of bed.</u> He and four other boys in his class had volunteered to clean up the town park. <u>It was just last week</u> that the sixth-graders were walking through the park and noticed the tangled weeds in the flower beds and <u>litter speckling the lawn like stars in the sky.</u> They spoke to their teacher and prinicipal, and with their support received permission to spend Friday afternoon doing their civic duty.

The writer describes what the character does as he thinks about the day's event.

This phrase helps the reader understand the sequence of events.

This description and simile help the reader visualize why the town park needs to be cleaned up.

Same Kind of Sentences

It was time for Anna to go home. She was tired. She had been working on the project all day. She had hardly made a dent in the work. She was the only one who could do the project on time. Anna was glad it was her last assignment.

Sentence Variety

Anna was tired and knew it was time to go home. Even though she had been working on the project all day, she had hardly made a dent in it. Was she really the only one who could get it done on time? She said quietly to herself, "I'm so glad this is my last assignment!"

Combine simple sentences using a compound verb.

Simple Sentences

Diego Rivera was a great muralist. He was from Mexico. He was a greatly respected artist.

Compound and Complex Sentences

Diego Rivera was a great muralist from Mexico whose work was greatly respected.

Use a variety of sentence beginnings.

Too Many Sentences Beginning the Same Way

Marisol was excited. Marisol was invited to the art opening. The art opening was at the museum. The museum normally only showed work by adults. The museum was having a special exhibit. The museum was featuring student artists' paintings and sculptures.

Varied Beginnings

Marisol was excited. She had been invited to the art opening at the museum. Normally, the museum only showed work by adults. This, however, was a special exhibit that featured the paintings and sculptures of student artists.

Conventions

Conventions are rules for grammar, spelling, punctuation, and capitalization. When you edit your writing, you check for conventions.

Conventions

- Always review your writing for spelling mistakes, even if you've used a computer spell checker.
- Check for capitalization in proper nouns and at the beginning of sentences.
- Check for correct end punctuation and use of commas in compound and complex sentences.
- Identify and correct sentence fragments and run-ons.

Editing Checklist

Use an editing checklist to review your writing.

_____ My writing has a clear introduction and conclusion.

_____ My ideas are well organized.

_____ My ideas are linked with words, phrases, and clauses.

_____ I have made specific word choices.

_____ I have checked for spelling mistakes.

_____ I have checked for correct use of capitalization and punctuation.

_____ I have included a variety of sentences.

_____ I have indented each paragraph.

Irregular Verbs

The past and past participle forms of irregular verbs are not formed by adding –ed or –d. Make sure to use the correct form of the verb.

Wrong Way	Right Way
I rung the bell to wake everyone up.	I rang the bell to wake everyone up.
Have you ever drank coconut juice?	Have you ever drunk coconut juice?

Coordinating Conjunctions

Use a comma and a coordinating conjunction *(for, and, nor, but, or, yet, so)* to combine two simple sentences into one compound sentence.

Wrong Way	Right Way
She enjoyed the book, the book took her a long time to read.	She enjoyed the book, <u>but</u> it took her a long time to read.
Melissa came in first place, Lucy came in second place.	Melissa came in first place, <u>and</u> Lucy came in second place.

Double Negatives

No, not, never, nowhere, nothing, nobody, no one, neither, and *barely* are examples of negatives. Use only one negative in a sentence.

Wrong Way	Right Way
My friend Drew hadn't never seen snow before.	My friend Drew hadn't ever seen snow before.
He says there isn't no better place than the beach.	He says there is no better place than the beach.

Direct Quotations

A direct quotation tells a speaker's exact words. Use quotation marks and a comma to set off a direct quotation from the rest of a sentence.

Wrong Way	Right Way
Vlad cried out That's not the way to handle the cat!	Vlad cried out, "That's not the way to handle the cat!"
I wish I could fly above the trees, said the baby sparrow.	"I wish I could fly above the trees," said the baby sparrow.

Writing Workshop

A **writing workshop** can help you get your revised draft ready to publish. In a writing workshop, you exchange your work with other students. They ask you questions and make suggestions to help you refine and edit your work. You do the same for them.

Asking Questions

- As you read your classmates' work, note any ideas you would like to know more about. Ask for clarification on those points.
- Do a quick check of capitalization, punctuation, spelling, and grammar. Sometimes it is easier for a new reader to find errors than for the writer to do so.
- Be polite! It can be hard to have your work criticized, so ask questions and offer suggestions in a constructive way.

Tapping the Earth

We have to find a way to heat and cool our homes without using gas or oil. In fact, we already have -- it's called geothermal heating and cooling. It uses pumps to bring the heat of the earth into homes in cold weather. It also uses the cooler temperatures of the earth to cool the indoors in hot weather. Many countries, such as Icelend, New zealand, and Turkey, already use geothermal systems for a lot of their heating and cooling. Unfortunately, it costs a lot to set up the system, but over time, lower utility bills will pay for it. In fact, homeowners would save between 30 percent and 70 percent of his total utility costs!

Peer Questions

- Can you define "geothermal"?
- Do you know how much it costs to set up a geothermal system?
- Can you tell more about where geothermal heating and cooling can be used?
- Are the names of the countries all spelled and capitalized correctly?
- Are your grammar and punctuation correct?

Another way to use a writing workshop is to collaborate. When you collaborate, you and other classmates work together to write one piece.

Collaboration

- Share ideas. Open your mind to new opinions.
- Share tasks. Each person in the group plays a role in getting the job done.
- Think about what you do best. How can you best help your group reach its goal?
- Stay on task. Do not allow the discussion to fall apart.
- Make sure everyone remembers the group's goal and works towards it.

How to Collaborate

Choose a reasonable topic. Ask
- What is the assignment?
- What do we already know about the topic?
- What do we still need to find out about the topic?
- Who might want to read about the topic?

Make the right choices. Ask
- How can we make our writing clearer?
- Have we chosen the best words to use?
- Do we need to add or cut any information?

Remember your chosen goal. Ask
- How do we feel about the finished work?
- Does it say everything we want it to say?
- Does it fulfill the assignment?

Using the Internet

Using your computer to research information can be a great help. The **Internet** provides many resources that you can access quickly and easily. Many Internet articles are also updated frequently, so the information is current.

Internet Research

- Before you search for information on unfamiliar websites, look for online encyclopedias or well-known newspapers.
- Before you take notes from a website, consider whether the site is a reliable source of information. Ask yourself: Is the writer an expert? What kind of bias might the writer have?
- Double-check personal websites or student-created sites for accuracy. Check with your teacher or librarian if you are not sure about the reliability of a site.
- Some newspaper articles, such as editorials, may tell opinions rather than facts.
- Remember to cite your source.

Parts of a Website

The *.org* in this URL tells me this is the website of an organization. Organizations may have expert information about a topic, but they may also have a bias.

| File | Edit | View | Favorites | Tools | Help |

Address http://www.---.org

WELCOME TO THE OFFICIAL PAGE OF THE ERIE ROLLERS!

LINKS

TEAM LINE-UP

SCHEDULE

ROLLER DERBY HISTORY

Meet Pennsylvania's coolest roller derby team! We have the best fans in the country. Check this site for the latest and greatest news about everyone's favorite skaters!

This is an official site, so this information about the team is probably reliable. I will still double-check it to be sure.

This sounds like an opinion.

If you're writing an opinion piece, it can be useful to visit websites that show opinions. You might get ideas for your own writing or find reasons to back up your own opinions. Remember that good opinion writing has both reasons and facts. Be sure to determine which information can be verified when you read a website.

File   Edit   View   Favorites   Tools   Help

Address   http://www.---.net/jmharrington.html

Weather in Florida

The weather in Florida is great. I think it's the best weather of any state in the United States. Florida is a subtropical climate with mild winters and warm, humid summers. The seasons are determined by the amount of rainfall rather than by temperature. Autumn and winter are the dry, pleasant seasons, while spring and summer are considered the wet, humid seasons.

If you take notes from a website, remember to cite your source!

Source: "Florida Weather." Facts for Fun in Florida, Web. July 2012. http://www.---.net

File   Edit   View   Favorites   Tools   Help

Address   http://www.---.com

DAILY GLOBE

REGION   U.S.   WORLD   SPORTS   ARTS   OP-ED

Bring in the Stadium!
JANUARY 6, 2013
Paul Samuels, Staff Reporter
My name is Paul Samuels, and I am the owner of a local sporting goods store. I believe that construction of the new baseball stadium will be very positive for our town. A lot of people are angry because they say the stadium will force people out of their homes, clog the streets with cars, and raise our taxes. I am going to explain why these ideas are not true.

Source: Samuels, Paul. "Bring in the Stadium!" Daily Globe, Web. 6 January 2013. http://www. ---. com

Writing for the Web

There are many ways to use technology to write. One way is to write for the web.

✏ E-mail

An e-mail is like a letter, but you can send it instantly to anyone in the world. E-mail can be friendly and personal when writing to a friend or family member. It can also be more formal when writing to someone you don't know very well, like in the example below.

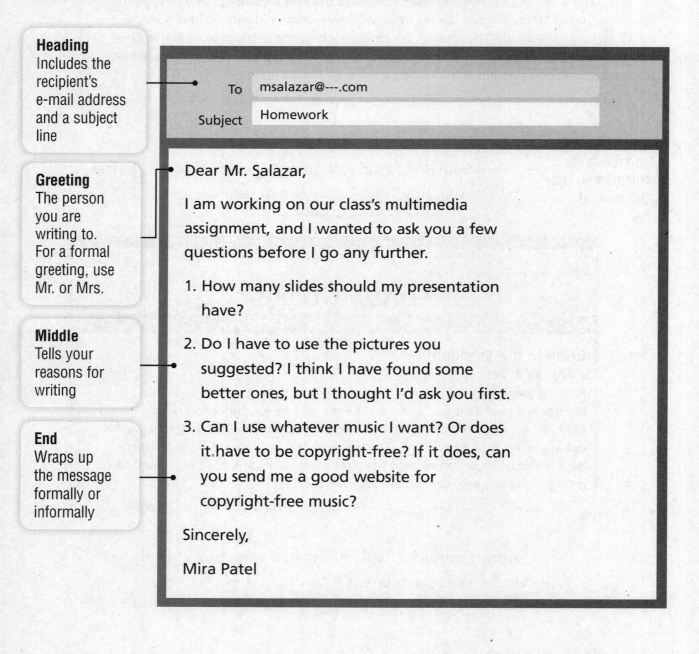

Heading
Includes the recipient's e-mail address and a subject line

Greeting
The person you are writing to. For a formal greeting, use Mr. or Mrs.

Middle
Tells your reasons for writing

End
Wraps up the message formally or informally

To   msalazar@---.com

Subject   Homework

Dear Mr. Salazar,

I am working on our class's multimedia assignment, and I wanted to ask you a few questions before I go any further.

1. How many slides should my presentation have?

2. Do I have to use the pictures you suggested? I think I have found some better ones, but I thought I'd ask you first.

3. Can I use whatever music I want? Or does it have to be copyright-free? If it does, can you send me a good website for copyright-free music?

Sincerely,

Mira Patel

Blog Post

Blog is short for "weblog." It is like a journal that you keep on the Internet. Other people can read and comment on it. Blog posts can be short, or they can be more like informative or persuasive essays.

URL

Blog Name

Post Title

Byline
Tells who wrote the post and when it was published

Body
Gives information, thoughts, and opinions

Comments
Left by readers

File   Edit   View   Favorites   Tools   Help

Address http://www.---.com/blog

Mr. Costello's 6th Grade Class Blog

Fashion is My Passion
by Olivia on May 13, 2012 at 2:00 P.M.

Some people think that how you present yourself is not important. They say it's what's on the inside that really counts. Well, I agree with that. But I love fashion, too. I think that the clothes you wear say a lot about who you are as a person.

I know that not everyone likes to dress up, but that's not what I mean. It's not what you wear, but how you wear it. If you really like the way you look, you will have a lot more confidence.

What I choose to wear depends on where I am going and what I am going to do there. At school, I have to wear my uniform, but I wear jeans and skirts and cute tops outside of school. I have a lot of funky jewelry, too. Your clothes can be a form of self-expression. Wearing interesting clothes makes me feel better about myself.

Do you think fashion is important? If so, why, and if it isn't, why not? I know everyone won't agree, but I want to hear what you think.

Comments (2)

Glen D:
Who you are on the inside is what really counts. I agree with that. You can't always judge a book by its cover.

Wanda X:
I consider myself pretty trendy. It's important to me that I look the way I want to. I don't think there is anything wrong with expressing yourself through your clothes. I wish we didn't have to wear uniforms to school, though—they are so plain!

Doing Research

The best way to support your informative or persuasive writing is to use facts and details. The best way to find facts and details is to do **research**.

Evaluating Sources

Sources are where you get your information. These include books, encyclopedias, periodicals, websites, and videos. Some sources are more reliable than others. How can you tell which sources are good? When looking at a new source, ask yourself these questions:

- Is the source published by experts in the field?
- If it is a website, is it trustworthy? *(Sites with .edu, .org, or .gov are educational, nonprofit, or government websites and can have good information.)*
- Is the source up-to-date? (It's important to have current facts, especially about science or current events.)
- Is the source relevant? Does it relate to your subject?

Primary vs. Secondary Sources

A primary source is first-hand information, usually from an eyewitness to an event. A secondary source includes information gathered by someone else. Here are some examples:

Primary Sources
- An interview with a scientist who studies earthquakes
- A journal entry by an earthquake survivor
- A survey of people who witnessed the earthquake

Secondary Sources
- A newspaper article about the earthquake
- An encyclopedia entry about earthquakes
- A TV documentary about the earthquake

Finding Books

Knowing your way around a library will make doing research easier. If you look for books in a library, you'll notice that every book has a number on its spine. This is the call number. Most libraries use the Dewey Decimal System to assign books call numbers. The numbers are based on 10 subject categories.

Dewey Decimal System

000–099 General Works

100–199 Philosophy

200–299 Religion

300–399 Social Sciences

400–499 Languages

500–599 Sciences

600–699 Technology

700–799 Arts and Recreation

800–899 Literature

900–999 History and Geography

Parts of a Title Page

Most of the information you need to cite a book is on its title page.

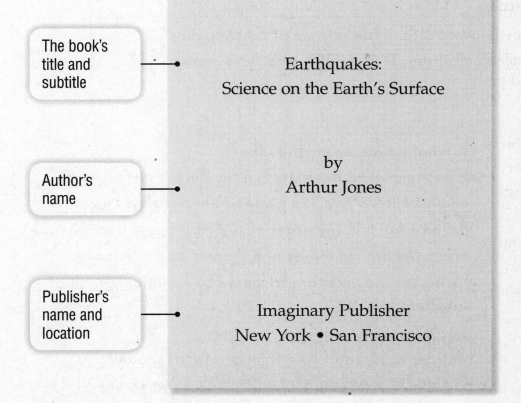

The book's title and subtitle

Author's name

Publisher's name and location

Earthquakes:
Science on the Earth's Surface

by
Arthur Jones

Imaginary Publisher
New York • San Francisco

Notetaking

When you gather information for a report or essay, you have to decide what information to include and how to organize it. As you research, take **notes** on note cards.

Note Cards

- Write a research question at the top of each card.
- You can write the answer by paraphrasing what the source says in your own words, copying a direct quote from the source, or writing a list with details from the source.
- Write the complete citation at the bottom of the card.

---

1. What causes an earthquake?

-- 20 plates on Earth's surface

-- space

-- the plates shift against each other

-- plate movement causes stress

-- stress is released as energy, which makes the ground

    move

Source: Wald, Lisa. "The Science of Earthquakes." US Geological Survey, 27 Oct 2009. Web. 4 November 2012.

List of details from the source.

Paraphrased information from the source.

Direct quote from the source.

1. What causes an earthquake?

It happens when two plates on the Earth's surface shift against each other. The place where the plates meet is called a fault. If the edges of the plates push against each other, the ground moves and there is an earthquake.

"Some earthquakes are triggered by explosive volcanic eruptions."

Source: Wald, Lisa. "The Science of Earthquakes." US Geological Survey, 27 Oct 2009. Web. 4 November 2012.

Keeping a Journal

Keeping a journal is another way to help with your notetaking. In a journal, you can express ideas, questions, thoughts, and feelings. This can help you later with your writing when you need to add to your main points or express your point of view.

Taking Notes in a Journal

- One way to take notes is to make two columns. Label one with the title of the text. Label the other Feelings and Responses.

- Read the text. In the left column, jot down quotations, ideas, and examples that confuse you, inspire you, or leave you asking questions. Include page numbers to refer back to the text.

- In the right column, jot down notes about the text. Include your feelings, thoughts, and any connections to the text you may have.

<u>Robotics</u> by Helena Domaine	Feelings and Responses
"These mechanical adventurers have computer brains that don't feel fear or panic." (634)	Ooh — this is some really strong language! It sets an exciting tone for the rest of the article.
"The science team had to call in a helicopter to rescue the robot." (635)	A helicopter? That sounds expensive.
"The Rovers also have a 'survival instinct' programmed into them." (636)	What's this "survival instinct"? I'd like to know more about this.
"The Swedish micro-bots are smaller than the hyphen between <u>micro</u> and <u>bots</u> in this sentence." (637)	Great description! I wonder what else can be that small.
-in 2003, robot soccer game at Carnegie Mellon University (638)	I would love to see this. Are there any games near my house?
-Bertram, robot butler (639)	This sounds funny. It reminds me of that old TV show.

Writing to a Prompt

Sometimes your teacher may give a timed writing assignment for a class exercise or a test. You will be given a **prompt** that asks you a question or tells you what to write about.

 ## Writing to a Prompt

- Look for key words that tell you what to do, such as explain, compare and contrast, convince or persuade, and summarize.
- Choose a focus, or main idea, for your writing.
- List and organize all your other ideas. Then add details, reasons, or facts to support your main idea.
- Spend about one-fourth of your time prewriting, half of your time drafting, and one-fourth of your time revising.

Sample Prompt:

Lewis and Clark's expedition to the West changed the United States. Think about how their expedition changed the United States. Write an essay explaining how their expedition changed the course of history in the United States.

Plan

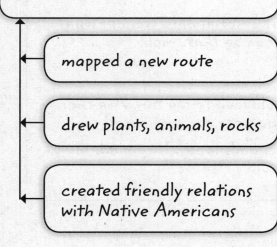

My focus: Lewis and Clark opened the American West when they traveled to the Pacific Ocean.

- mapped a new route
- drew plants, animals, rocks
- created friendly relations with Native Americans

Draft

The westward expedition headed by Meriwether Lewis and William Clark opened up the land and the resources of the West to the whole country. Between 1803 and 1806, Lewis and Clark traveled from Pittsburgh to the Pacific Ocean. Their aims were to plan a route and report on what they saw along the way. They mapped a route across the country. In addition, they described and drew plants, animals, and geologic formations that they saw. Most important, they created friendly relations with Native Americans, which helped later groups to make the same trip more safely.

Types of Writing Prompts

There are different types of writing prompts that you may be asked to complete. Here are some of those types:

Narrative Prompt	Persuasive Prompt
Asks you to recount a personal or fictional experience or tell a story based on a real or imagined event	Asks you to convince the reader that your point of view is valid or that the reader should take a specific action
Informative Prompt	**Response to Literature**
Asks you to explain why or how, to clarify a process, or to define a concept	Asks you to answer questions about something you read

Narrative Prompt:

In the near future, space travel might be accessible for everyone—not just astronauts.

Suppose you were to have an opportunity to travel into space.

Write a story describing your experience.

Persuasive Prompt:

The post office honors people by putting them on stamps.

Choose a person from history who you think should be on a stamp.

Write a letter to persuade the United States Postal Service to use that person's image on a new stamp.

Informative Prompt:

There are many environmental issues that cause concern.

Think of an environmental issue that concerns you.

Write a paragraph that describes the issue and offers a possible solution.

Response to Literature Prompt:

Every novel shows an author's point of view.

Think of your favorite novel.

Write a paragraph explaining the author's point of view in this novel.

Checklists and Rubrics

Use this rubric to evaluate your writing. Circle a number in each column to rate your writing. Then revise your writing to improve your score.

	• Focus • Support	• Organization
Score 6	My writing is focused and supported by facts or details.	My writing has a clear introduction and conclusion. Ideas are clearly organized.
Score 5	My writing is mostly focused and supported by facts or details.	My writing has an introduction and a conclusion. Ideas are mostly organized.
Score 4	My writing is mostly focused and supported by some facts or details.	My writing has an introduction and a conclusion. Most ideas are organized.
Score 3	Some of my writing is focused and supported by some facts or details.	My writing has an introduction or a conclusion but might be missing one. Some ideas are organized.
Score 2	My writing is not focused and is supported by few facts or details.	My writing might not have an introduction or a conclusion. Few ideas are organized.
Score 1	My writing is not focused or supported by facts or details.	My writing is missing an introduction and a conclusion. Few or no ideas are organized.

Elaboration • Purpose	Conventions • Evidence • Development
Purpose is strongly conveyed throughout. Writing grabs readers' interest. Word choice strongly conveys tone.	My writing has no errors in spelling, grammar, capitalization, or punctuation. Writing includes description, details, and/or reasons.
Purpose is explained at the beginning and end. Writing holds readers' interest. Most word choices convey tone.	My writing has few errors in spelling, grammar, capitalization, or punctuation. Writing includes much description, details, and/or reasons.
Purpose is explained at the beginning or end of text. Overall writing holds readers' interest. Many word choices convey tone.	My writing has some errors in spelling, grammar, capitalization, or punctuation. Writing includes some description, details, and/or reasons.
Purpose is somewhat explained. Overall writing holds readers' interest, but needs more description. Several word choices convey tone.	My writing has some errors in spelling, grammar, capitalization, or punctuation. Writing includes a few examples of description, details, and/or reasons.
Some attempt to explain purpose. Writing holds reader's interest in places. A few word choices convey tone.	My writing has many errors in spelling, grammar, capitalization, or punctuation. There is little variety of sentences. Some sentences are incomplete.
Purpose is unclear. Writing lacks interest. Tone does not support type of writing.	My writing has many errors in spelling, grammar, capitalization, or punctuation. There is no variety of sentences. Sentences are incomplete.

Cause-Effect Essay

A **cause-effect essay** describes something that happened (the effect) and explains how a person, object, or event made it happen (the cause).

Parts of a Cause-Effect Essay

- A topic sentence that introduces a cause, an effect, or both
- Details that explain the causes
- Details that describe the effects
- Transition words or phrases that connect ideas
- An ending that ties together ideas

Hurricane Katrina

Introduction
Contains a topic sentence that introduces the effect

Hurricane Katrina was one of the worst natural disasters ever to hit the United States. It caused about $81 billion in damage and killed nearly 2,000 people. Other hurricanes have had stronger winds or produced more rainfall, but for several reasons, Katrina was worse than any of them.

Body
Gives details that show several causes and effects

To understand why, you have to know how hurricanes form. They develop over tropical oceans, where the water temperature is at least 80 degrees and the air holds a lot of moisture. As the air rises, it cools, and the air pressure drops. The result is a cluster of rainstorms, with wind rushing in a circle around the low-pressure area. If the wind speed reaches 75 miles per hour, weather scientists call it a hurricane.

Other Transitions
Caused
Reasons
Why
Result
Because
Due to
So
Led

More causes lead to effects

On August 23, 2005, Katrina formed in the Atlantic Ocean east of Florida. Because hurricanes are fed by moisture, it lost strength as it passed over Florida. But it quickly regained hurricane strength as it passed over the Gulf of Mexico.

These two paragraphs give details about the causes that led to the effects described.

The waters in the Gulf were unusually warm that year. The pressure of the atmosphere at the center of the storm was among the lowest ever recorded. Due to these conditions, wind speeds increased to over 175 miles per hour. These swirling winds caused the storm to double in size. By the time Katrina reached Louisiana, on the morning of August 29, it was one of the most powerful storms to hit the United States in the last 100 years.

The city of New Orleans, Louisiana, lay directly in the path of the hurricane. The storm dumped 8 to 15 inches of rain on parts of Louisiana. The wind and surging seas caused boats and cars to ram into buildings. In New Orleans, the storm caused Lake Pontchartrain to overflow. Before Katrina, a system of walls, called levees, was designed to hold back the waters. During the storm, many levees broke under the pressure of the water because they had been poorly built. In all, 53 levees in the New Orleans area failed, with the result that 80 percent of the city was underwater.

Ending Shows the final effect and wraps up the ideas of the essay

The floods caused thousands of people to be stranded for days without food or clean water. Many of them took shelter in a football stadium, but others were trapped on roofs, and many drowned. There was plenty of warning about the storm, but roads became clogged with traffic, so cars could not move. In the days after the storm, the Coast Guard rescued about 33,500 people. The U.S. government, other states, private charities, and even other countries sent aid. A lot of blame went around for the slow response to the storm and for the poorly built levees.

We can't control nature. But Hurricane Katrina led the country to resolve to be better prepared for natural disasters.

Problem-Solution Essay

A **problem-solution essay** states a problem and suggests at least one way to solve the problem.

Parts of a Problem-Solution Essay

- An introduction that states the problem
- Details and examples that make the problem clear
- One or more reasonable solutions, with details that explain them
- Transition words that link examples and signal solutions

Clean Up Gross Park

Introduction
Explains the problem

Everyone knows the trash-filled strip of grass on Hill Street, on the border between the towns of Florence and Sparta. Everyone calls it Gross Park. Because it is right on the border, neither town takes responsibility for it. As a result, the grass is never mowed. All kinds of trash and debris collect there. People walk their dogs there and don't bother to clean up after them. It has become a health hazard. Both towns blame each other for the problem, but the solution is simple. Both towns should work together to clean up Gross Park.

A possible solution is introduced.

First, we could call a meeting to discuss the solution. We could meet at the community center. At the meeting, people could discuss different things we can do to make the park a nice place. Step two would be to choose a Saturday and organize a volunteer crew to clean up the park. People could offer to bring lawn mowers and other tools. Everyone could chip in a little money to buy heavy work gloves.

Details explain the solution.

Other Transitions
To begin
Also
Secondly
Meanwhile
The final step

Once the park is cleaned up, we would need to decide what to do with the space. Everyone who takes part in the cleanup, children and adults, could have a vote. It's too small for soccer, but there's enough space that we could put a basketball court in the south end, near the school, and people could use the north end for a community garden. Those are just my ideas, and other people might have better ones.

These paragraphs further develop the solution.

Some improvements to the park will likely cost money. So the next step would be to research how much money different ideas would cost. We would decide to make changes that are fun but not too expensive. Then, we could hold a community fundraiser to help us turn Gross Park into a place that both towns will enjoy.

Conclusion
Summarizes and reinforces the solution

How do we know that people won't keep dumping garbage in the park? After all, it has been Gross Park for years. People will respect the space because of the hard work they did to change it. They will see it as a real park, not a dump. If we make the effort, Gross Park will become Clean Park.

Note how the author of this piece:

- Included reasonable solutions.

  We would decide to make changes that are fun but not too expensive.

- Addressed possible concerns of readers.

  How do we know that people won't keep dumping garbage in the park?... People will respect the space because of the hard work they did to change it.

Compare-Contrast Essay

A **compare-contrast essay** tells how two or more people, places, or things are alike and how they are different.

Parts of a Compare-Contrast Essay

- An introduction that states the main idea
- A body that is organized logically: similarities first, then differences; differences, then similarities; or similarities and differences point by point
- Transition words that indicate similarities and differences
- Supporting sentences that explain similarities and differences
- A conclusion that sums up the essay

The Chimp's Smaller Cousin

Introduction
Tells what topic the essay will compare and contrast

Until 1954, the bonobo used to be called the pygmy chimpanzee. Scientists labeled them as separate species, but bonobos look so much like common chimps that bonobos' smaller size was the only noticeable difference. However, the more scientists have studied the bonobo, the more differences they have noted between the two species.

Body
Describes similarities, then differences

Most people would have trouble telling the chimp and bonobo apart. Both have dark faces, long black hair, and wide nostrils. They both have long, powerful arms for climbing and moving around in trees. They both walk upright when carrying things with their hands and arms. Both chimps and bonobos are social with their own species, using facial expressions

This paragraph compares the two species.

and hand gestures to communicate. Chimp and bonobo females alike begin to have babies at ages 12 to 14, and they nurse and carry their young for three to five years.

Other Transitions
On one hand
On the other hand
Like
Unlike
Both
Also
Similarly

These paragraphs contrast the two species.

The differences between the species show themselves both in the wild and in zoos. The bonobo is shorter and thinner than the chimp, but its limbs are longer in proportion to its body. Its natural habitat is the rainforest, while the chimp is at home in several habitats. That may explain why the bonobo spends more of its time in trees than chimps do, even in zoos. When it is on the ground, the bonobo spends more time walking upright than the chimp does, and less time "knuckle-walking" on all fours. Bonobos eat mostly fruit, though sometimes they hunt monkeys and other small animals. Chimps by contrast eat a lot of meat and often organize hunting parties. Chimps have been observed using tools to get food, such as sticks to dig up insects. Bonobos never do this in the wild, but they have learned how to do it in zoos.

There are also social differences between the two species. An "alpha male" usually controls a community of chimps. He makes himself the boss by threatening the others. Females, on the other hand, lead bonobos. They make peace among the males and form alliances to control them. There may be an alpha male in a bonobo community, but his rank among other males is determined by his mother's rank.

Conclusion Sums up the essay

Scientists think that the two species separated from each other less than one million years ago. In the wild, in Africa, chimpanzees only live north of the Congo River while bonobos live south of the river. Both species are poor swimmers and don't like to swim. It is likely that when the river formed, about one and a half to two million years ago, the two groups were separated from each other and developed in different ways. In time, changes in their genes resulted in separate species.

Unfortunately, one last thing bonobos and chimps have in common is that they are both endangered species. Scientists are making efforts to help both species survive.

How-to Essay

A **how-to essay** gives a step-by-step explanation of how something is done.

Parts of a How-to Essay

- An introduction that describes the topic
- A list of materials needed
- Transitions that present the steps in a clear order
- Relevant facts that explain reasons for steps
- A concluding statement that wraps up the main ideas

How to Make Marbled Eggs

Introduction Describes the topic

When my family came to the United States, we discovered the American custom of coloring eggs. In my native country, Indonesia, we have a tradition of coloring eggs too, but it is not connected with a holiday. We do it to make our dinner pretty and more fun to eat! We call it *telur berwarna*, which in English means "marbled eggs."

It's easy to make telur berwarna. It takes about two and a half hours, but most of that is just waiting time. You'll need:

A list of materials tells readers what they will need.

- Water
- 6 eggs
- Salt
- Small pot
- Wooden spoon
- 3 small saucepans
- Red, green, and yellow food coloring

Other Transitions
Start
Then
During
Once
While
Next
Later
Last

Transition words show steps in order.

To start, take the eggs out of the refrigerator and let them come to room temperature. Put them in a small pot carefully so that you don't crack the shells. Cover with cold water and add salt. Then heat the water gently—don't let it boil! During the first five minutes, keep stirring with the handle of a wooden spoon to make sure the yolks stay in the middle.

Body
Explains steps in the process as well as reasons for the steps

Once the water is bubbling gently, cook for about seven more minutes. Then remove the pot from the stove. Carefully pour the hot water into the sink. Then quickly run cold water over the eggs. This is to make sure the eggs don't stick to the insides of the shells.

While the eggs are cooling, fill three small saucepans with water and add food coloring, one color to each. Put in enough food coloring to give the water a deep, rich color. Then bring the saucepans to a heavy boil.

Next, tap each egg on a hard surface. This is the tricky step. You want to tap hard enough to crack the shells, but not hard enough to break off any part of them. Using the wooden spoon, put two eggs in each of the saucepans and simmer for another five minutes. Then turn off the heat and allow the eggs to cool in the colored water for at least two hours.

Later, peel the eggs. They should have a bright, marbled color. The last step is the best: Serve the eggs and eat them! They taste just like regular hard-boiled eggs, but they're prettier and more fun to eat.

Conclusion
Suggests some uses for the finished product

In Indonesia, we usually serve telur berwarna cut in halves on top of sticky yellow rice seasoned with fried onion, coconut, and spices. But you can serve it lots of different ways. Try it on top of a green salad, or turn it into an egg-salad sandwich. If you bring it to school in your lunchbox, though, be warned that your friends will want to trade for it!

Explanation Essay

An **explanation essay** tells how or why a process works.

Parts of an Explanation Essay

- An introduction that states the topic
- A step-by-step description of the process
- Supporting details to make the steps clear
- A conclusion that summarizes the explanation

Introduction
States the topic

Body
Explains the steps of the process

Building a Guitar

A handcrafted musical instrument is more than just a tool for someone to make nice sounds on. It's a work of art in itself. Take a guitar, for example. Most guitars are made in factories, but a handmade one is something special. There are dozens of steps involved in building one, and most builders will take the trouble to make it look and sound beautiful.

Building a guitar starts with the wood. Guitar makers choose blocks of wood carefully. They keep them in their workshops and saw off pieces as they need them. Some say they only use wood from trees that they cut themselves!

Different kinds of wood are used for different parts. The top is most important. It's made of spruce. It has a fine, even grain that produces the best sound. The sides, back, and neck may be made of rosewood, mahogany, or different kinds of maple. The fingerboard, below the strings, is usually made of ebony. That's a very hard wood that lasts a long time.

Other Transitions
Starts
Before
First
Then
Lastly
After
Next
Finally

Supporting details include further explanation of the steps and reasons for them.

Before cutting the top, the guitar maker first marks off the round hole in the middle. She uses special tools to cut the hole and the fancy pattern around it. Then she uses a kind of saw called a pin router to cut the wood into the guitar shape. Lastly, she glues small pieces of wood to the inside part to make it stronger.

Transition words point out the steps.

A machine called a bending jig is used to shape the sides. It has a metal part that is heated by electricity and is in the exact shape of the side of a guitar. First, a strip of wood is soaked in hot water so that it will bend without breaking. Then it is clamped tightly to the bending jig and heated for a few minutes. After it cools, it is unclamped from the machine. Amazingly, it holds its shape.

Next the builder uses a special kind of glue to put the top, sides, and back together. So far, all the steps are something that any skilled carpenter could do. But now comes the part that turns these pieces of wood into a musical instrument. The builder cuts grooves in the neck where the frets will go. Those are the metal strips that the guitar player's fingers will hold against the strings. If they are not in exactly the right places, the guitar won't play in tune! The same goes for the bridge, the strip at the bottom where the ends of the strings are fastened. The place where it goes has to be marked just right if the guitar is going to sound good.

Now it's starting to look like a guitar. The next step is to seal and lacquer the wood so that it looks pretty—and so that the wood will last. The builder pounds the frets into the neck with a mallet and then glues the neck and bridge to the body. Finally, the pegs and strings are put in.

Conclusion Wraps up the explanation

Now we're ready for some music! Most people admire a person who plays the guitar well. But let's have some respect for the person who knew the right way to build it!

Classification Essay

A **classification essay** explains a topic by discussing its parts.

Parts of a Classification Essay

- An introduction that presents the topic
- A brief summary that lists the parts of the topic
- An explanation of each part
- A conclusion that summarizes or restates the main points

Mollusks

Introduction Presents the topic

Mollusks are a large group of animals that mostly live in the sea. There are five main groups of mollusks, and they all look so different that it's hard to imagine that they could be related. Most mollusks have three main body parts. They have a head, but not all species have brains. In those that do, the brain is wrapped around the tube that takes in food!

These sentences describe what is similar about the parts being classified.

That's in a central part that contains most of the animal's body organs. There's also a foot that they use for movement. All mollusks have a fold of skin called a mantle. In some species, the mantle forms a shell.

There are about 85,000 known species of mollusks. The biggest group, with about 70,000 species, is the snails and slugs. A slug is really a snail without a shell. This is the only group with species that can breathe air and live on land.

Other Transitions
Five main groups
All
Most
Biggest
Second-biggest
Most interesting
Most unusual

Body paragraphs Explain each part

The second-biggest group, with about 9,000 species, is the bivalves. These are the familiar "shellfish" such as clams, oysters, and mussels. Of course, they're not really fish. Most species live in the sea, but some live in fresh water. "Bivalve" means "two doors."

These animals have a hinge that can open their two shells for eating and close them to keep from being eaten.

The chitons are a group of about 1,000 species. Their hard shells are made up of eight flexible plates. They live and feed not far from the shore. When they die, the plates come apart. They wash up on beaches, where people sometimes mistake them for parts of lobsters.

Each body paragraph includes facts and examples.

The most interesting group of mollusks includes the squids and octopuses. There are about 800 species, but fossils show that there used to be many more. In these animals, the muscular foot branches into tentacles. They are the only group in which all species are meat eaters. They all can squirt ink to protect themselves from predators, and they can change color in less than a second. They are the largest of all the invertebrates (animals without backbones), and the giant squid is the largest of all. They have the biggest brains and the best-developed senses of all mollusks. Unlike other mollusks, they are social animals. They like to hang out together. When others of their species aren't around, they may even travel with schools of fish.

The fifth main group is the most unusual. They're sometimes called "sea cucumbers," and there are about 200 species. They have no shells and look something like short, fat worms. Until recently, scientists didn't know they were mollusks at all. They thought they were more closely related to starfish. But their digestive system is like other mollusks'.

Conclusion Wraps up the main idea and facts

Mollusks show us that you can't always tell what group an animal belongs to just by looking at it. In fact, their body plans are so different that it's hard for scientists to find characteristics that describe all of them. But their DNA— their genes—shows that they are related after all.

Definition Essay

A **definition essay** explains the meaning of a word or phrase.

Parts of a Definition Essay

- An introduction that defines the word or phrase
- Opinions and details that support and explain the definition
- Often an opinion statement that expresses the writer's views
- A conclusion that wraps up the definition and examples

What Is Technology?

Introduction
Defines the word and states the writer's opinion

When people think of the word "technology," they usually have in mind a gadget like a computer or a smart phone. But technology is more than that. It is what you get when science is made useful by people and for people. The dictionary defines it as the making and using of tools to solve a problem or to do a job. But I think technology is even more than that. I think that it is one of the things that makes us human, like language and walking on two legs. It's how we make our lives better and more comfortable.

Let's start with Stone Age people. They didn't invent fire. But they saw it all around them, such as when lightning struck a forest or when a volcano erupted. At some point, they must have figured out that the scary, dangerous flames could cook their food and keep them warm. That was an early example of science. When they figured out how to control and make fire, that was technology.

Other Transitions
For example
For instance
In this case
However
To conclude
As I have said

Body
Gives examples and details that support the definition

The same thing happened when people discovered all the things they could do with rocks. They must have observed that rocks were hard the first time someone stubbed his or her toe on one. But figuring out that they could shape those hard things to do all kinds of useful jobs was technology. Have you ever seen a picture of a Stone Age hand axe? I think it was a more important invention than the smart phone.

Let's jump ahead a few hundred thousand years to a more recent example. Ben Franklin proved that lightning was electricity with his famous kite experiment. Later, scientists figured out what electricity is and how to control it. But it was technology developed by people like Thomas Edison that made all the useful things that are powered by electric currents, such as lights and radios.

There are all kinds of technology. There is computer technology that helps us communicate. There is medical technology that helps save lives. Last but not least, there's simple technology like spoons and screwdrivers that we don't think about because they are so ordinary. But someone had to figure out how to make and use them, and other people had to figure out how to make them better.

This paragraph argues against views that are different from the writer's.

Some people seem to think technology is bad. They like to point out that a lot of technology goes into making more and more powerful weapons. They look at cars and see pollution. They look at new machines and talk about how they put people out of work. That's all true, but I just can't understand how people can think that way. You could just as well say talking is bad because people gossip and tell lies.

Conclusion
Wraps up the definition and examples

The best thing about technology is that it is always changing. As we learn more about the world, we can make even better technology that helps even more people. That's the human way.

Interview

An **interview** is a question-and-answer session with a person to find out interesting information. An interview will usually answer the questions *who, what, where, when, why,* and *how.*

Parts of an Interview

- Facts and opinions that make the person interviewed an interesting subject
- A list of questions to ask, and the interviewee's answers
- A concluding question to wrap up the interview

Identify the subject and what you know about him or her.

Prepare a list of questions in advance.

Write down the answers. If you want to tape or video record the interview, ask permission first.

Rick Ramirez,
Hiker on the Pacific Crest Trail

Rick, you recently finished hiking the Pacific Crest Trail, from Mexico to Canada. What made you take on such a challenge?

Well, I've always enjoyed hiking. When I was a kid, my family often took camping vacations. A lot of our hikes were on parts of the Pacific Crest Trail, and I decided when I was 12 that someday I would hike the whole thing.

How long is the whole thing?

It's 2,663 miles.

How long did it take you to hike that far?

It took me most of two summers, 2010 and 2011. Some people try to hike the whole trail in one season, but because I was in college, I had to split it up.

A hike like that must take a lot of training and preparation. What did you do to get ready?

Well, you have to be in pretty good shape to start. I ran cross-country in high school and college, and I practiced running uphill a lot. I'd go to an office building and run up the stairs to the 42nd floor. Sometimes I wore a 60-pound backpack. I sure got a lot of strange looks!

How did you find food on the trail? Did you have to forage?

You mean like a bear? *(laughs)* Sometimes I ate things like huckleberries that grew near the trail. But no, I carried a backpacking stove and prepared food caches. You send food packages to yourself at post offices along the trail, and there are tiny towns here and there where you can resupply. I had the best meal of my life at a mountain lodge in Oregon, just over the line from California. It's mainly for skiers, and in July we had the restaurant almost to ourselves. Did we ever eat!

You say "we." So you had company on your hike?

For most of it, yes. I had friends who joined me for maybe a week or so at a time. That was another way I got food, having friends bring it when we met up. You also make friends with other hikers along the trail. There weren't very many days that I was entirely by myself.

Did you run into any danger?

If you mean like wild animals or falling off a mountain, no, not really. I've had encounters with bears on other trips, but amazingly not on this one. There were times I was very uncomfortable, though. There are stretches where you have to go 20 miles between sources of water. That can get a little hairy, especially at the southern end of the trail, when you go through the desert. Then as you go north, you have to put up with a lot of rain and cold nights.

Would you ever do it again?

In a heartbeat. But there are other trails I want to try first.

Thank you for your time, Rick.

My pleasure.

Be ready to change the questions or their order depending on the answers you get.

Ask a concluding question to wrap up the interview.

Be polite, listen carefully, and say thank you.

News Story

A **news story** gives information about a current event, an issue, or a person.

Parts of a News Story

- A headline that tells what the story is about
- A lead that contains the most important facts about the story
- A body containing facts and details that support the lead

Headline
Introduces the story

Lead
Gives the most important facts telling *who*, *what*, *where*, *when*, and *why*

Body
Tells *how* and supports the lead with details

Sixth Grader Wants Student Representative on School Board

Elly Chou, a 6th-grade student at Nichols Middle School, is sponsoring a bill in the city council this year that would put a student representative on the Board of Education because she thinks politicians don't pay attention to student concerns.

Last fall, Elly, the 6th-grade class president at Nichols, wrote to the board protesting cuts in art and music programs. When she received no answer, she decided it was because board members don't think students' opinions matter.

"They listen to our parents because they pay taxes," Elly explained. "They listen to our teachers, but they think they can ignore us kids. Aren't we what school is all about?"

With the help of Marc Hogan, a lawyer and the husband of Elly's 5th-grade teacher, Elly wrote a bill proposing that students be allowed to elect a representative to the board. The student representative would sit in on board meetings and give opinions but would not have a vote. The bill comes up for consideration in the city council this Tuesday.

Would Elly like to be the student representative if her bill passes? "Someday," she says, grinning, "but I guess it should be someone in high school."

Survey: Social Studies

A **survey** is a set of questions or choices given to a group of people to find out what they think about a subject or issue.

Parts of a Survey

- An introduction that explains the issue
- A request for answers
- A set of questions or choices

Introduction
Explains the topic

A call to action is made.

Body
Lists the choices

Nichols School Party Survey

The party committee is starting to make plans for the end-of-the-school year celebration. In previous years, the committee has chosen the theme of the party, but this year, the whole student body will choose the theme.

Please help make this decision. Indicate your choice by checking the box next to the party theme you most like.

❑ **Undersea Adventure:** A blue-water theme with sea creatures, a shipwreck, pirate treasure chest and so on. This would go well with our school mascot, the Dolphins.

❑ **King Arthur's Court:** A Middle Ages theme with the gym decorated like a castle for all you knights and damsels. There might even be a dragon to tame.

❑ **Sixties Sensations:** Enter the world of your grandparents' youth! There will be beads, bright colors, and of course the music of the Beatles, the Temptations, and other golden oldies.

❑ **To the Sky...and Beyond!:** A journey through outer space aboard a starship, with appropriate decorations from across the galaxy.

Business Letter

A **business letter** is a letter that is written to someone the writer does not know well. It is more formal than a friendly letter. People often write business letters when they want to request something.

Parts of a Business Letter

- A heading, an inside address, and a salutation that includes the recipient's title
- An opening sentence that makes the purpose of the letter clear
- Supporting sentences that add details
- A polite closing and signature

The heading gives the writer's address and the date.

The inside address tells to whom the letter is being sent.

The salutation uses titles such as *Mr.* or *Ms.*

Details tell how the letter's recipient can best help the writer.

Closing and Signature

1633 SW 72nd Avenue
Plantation, FL 33321
March 18, 2012

Dr. Marjorie Harris
Oceanview Pet Clinic
6101 McCall Street
Lauderdale-by-the Sea, FL 33308

Dear Dr. Harris:

   I would like some information about how to become a veterinarian. I know that I need to go to college and take lots of science classes, but I have a few more questions. First of all, I am interested in taking care of zoo animals when I grow up. I am also interested in taking care of cats and dogs. Is it possible to do both, or do I have to choose? Secondly, are there summer camps or after school classes that can teach kids about animals? Finally, can you recommend any books that would help me? I would appreciate any advice. Thank you for your time.

Sincerely,

Shamira Richardson

Science Observation Report

A **science observation report** uses narrative writing to describe the procedure and results of an experiment or process in science.

Parts of a Science Observation Report

- A statement that tells what the observation is about
- Details that show what happened and when
- A summary of what was learned

May 14

Evaporation Experiment

Purpose:

Purpose
Introduces the project

We filled two identical glass measuring cups with water to the 500-ml mark. We placed one near the windows and the other on the lab table on the far side of the room. Our class is going to observe which evaporates faster.

Observations:

MAY 15

Observations
Gives dates and records what happened

2:00. Sunny day. Water levels in both cups are already lower. The one near the windows is at 470 ml, and the one far from the window is at 495 ml.

MAY 16

2:00. Overcast day. Water level in cup near windows at 450 ml. Level in cup on lab table is at 490 ml. Both cups have a layer of white scum where water has evaporated.

MAY 18

2:00. Sunny day. Water level in cup near windows at 390 ml, cup on table at 450 ml.

Conclusions
Summarizes what was learned

Conclusions: I learned that water evaporates faster when exposed to direct sunlight. I also learned that our water has a lot of dissolved minerals.

Research Report

A **research report** closely examines a topic or idea. It uses factual information gathered from several sources.

Parts of a Research Report

- An introduction that clearly states the topic
- Body paragraphs with main ideas and supporting details
- Facts and examples as supporting details
- A conclusion that sums up the main points

Introduction
States the main topic

Body Paragraphs
Use details to support the main ideas

Facts, examples, and direct quotes support the main idea.

The Changing Arctic

Introduction

The Arctic is known for its extremely cold climate. Its warmest month, July, has average temperatures below 50°F. Winter temperatures can fall to −40°F. However, in recent decades, the average temperatures have risen, and the Arctic ice caps have begun to melt.

The Melting Ice Cap

Data show parts of the Arctic have warmed by 4° to 5°F since 1950 (Arctic Science Magazine, Sept. 28, 2011). Now, 5 degrees may not seem like much. But in the Arctic, sea temperatures hover right around freezing. Just a few degrees one way or the other can make the difference between ice and water.

During all seasons of the year, but especially in summer, the Arctic ice cap is much smaller than it was even 30 years ago (NOAA graph). It has lost about one million square miles—a greater area than all the United States east of the Mississippi River. Though it is hard for scientists to measure the thickness of Arctic sea ice, scientists have found lots of "data to suggest that the ice is thinning as well as shrinking in area" (Arctic Science Magazine).

What it Means for Wildlife

Melting sea ice has already affected wildlife. Polar bears are losing their habitat. They feed mainly by hunting seals from floating ice. Summer is the time they fatten up, and they now have to migrate farther and farther in search of food. In 2009, wildlife experts found that of the world's 19 polar bear populations, eight are listed as threatened species. Experts fear that two-thirds of the world's polar bears could disappear by 2050 (Polar Bear Info Online).

Walruses are also losing their habitat. After fishing for clams and other animals at the bottom of the sea, walruses usually get tired and rest on ice caps. As the ice caps melt, walruses swim closer to the shore of Alaska. Some migrate to Russia. The habitat in those areas cannot handle large numbers of walruses, and many of the baby walruses end up dying (Arctic Science Magazine).

Conclusion

Though the Arctic is still one of the coldest areas on Earth, its temperature has risen. As the ice caps begin to melt, polar bears, walruses, and other animals lose their habitat.

Citations show where information was found.

Conclusion Sums up the report

Note how the author of this piece:

- Used headings to organize sections of the report. For example, the information found under "The Melting Ice Cap" relates to how the shape of the Arctic has changed because of melting.

- Used various sources for his information, including magazines, websites, and graphs. This writer also included the date of the magazine article he used.

Graphs, Diagrams, and Charts

Graphs, diagrams, and charts are helpful for showing data and making comparisons. A report or summary can be made even better through the use of these types of graphic organizers.

Graphs and Charts
Are used to compare or to show how something changes over time

Line Graphs
Use straight lines in a grid to show how many or how much

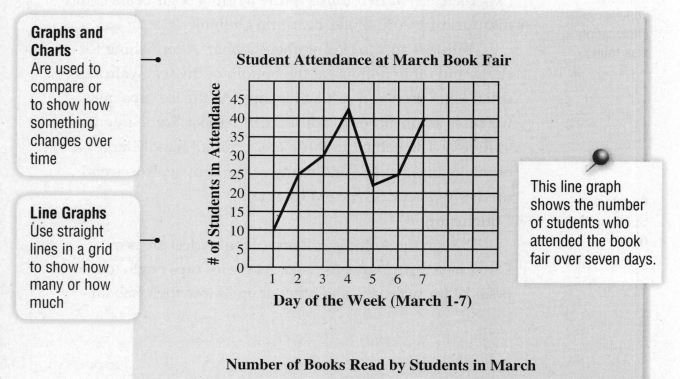

Student Attendance at March Book Fair

# of Students in Attendance

Day of the Week (March 1-7)

This line graph shows the number of students who attended the book fair over seven days.

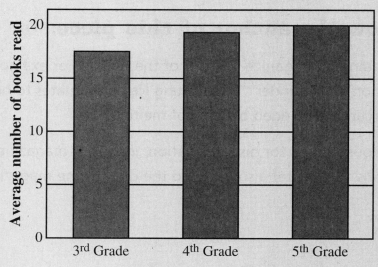

Number of Books Read by Students in March

Average number of books read

3rd Grade   4th Grade   5th Grade

Students Participating in the Reading Contest

Pie Charts
Work best
for showing
percentages

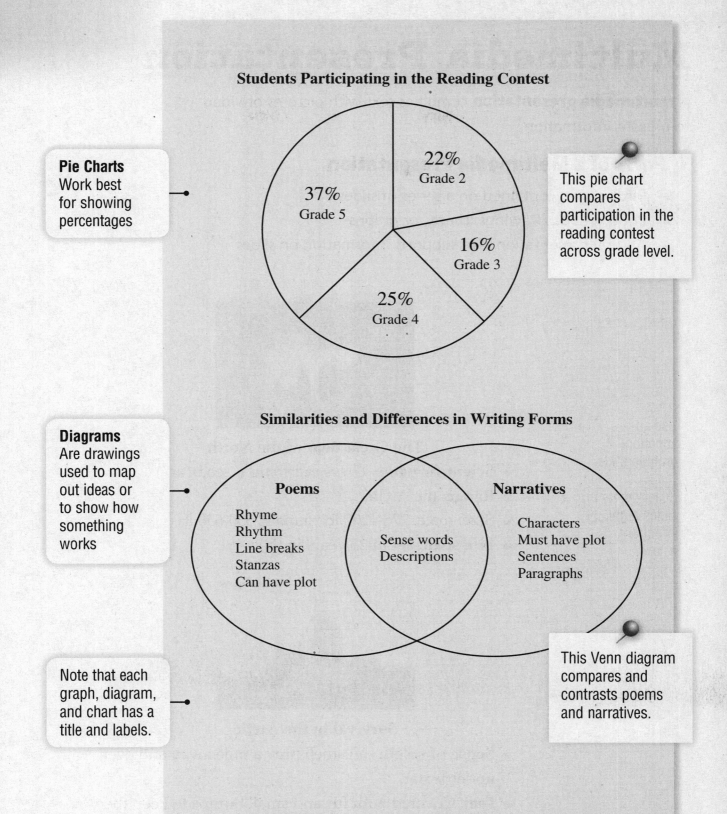

22%
Grade 2

37%
Grade 5

16%
Grade 3

25%
Grade 4

This pie chart
compares
participation in the
reading contest
across grade level.

Similarities and Differences in Writing Forms

Diagrams
Are drawings
used to map
out ideas or
to show how
something
works

Poems

Rhyme
Rhythm
Line breaks
Stanzas
Can have plot

Sense words
Descriptions

Narratives

Characters
Must have plot
Sentences
Paragraphs

This Venn diagram
compares and
contrasts poems
and narratives.

Note that each
graph, diagram,
and chart has a
title and labels.

Multimedia Presentation

A **multimedia presentation** combines text with pictures or video to present information.

✏️ Parts of a Multimedia Presentation

- Information contained on a series of slides
- Photographs, drawings, charts, or graphs
- An oral presentation that supports information on slides

> Use an attention-grabbing title.

> Bullet points on slides highlight important details.

The Great Bear of the North

- **Scientific name**: *Ursus maritimus* ("sea bear")
- **Range:** the Arctic
- **Size:** male, 775-1200 lb.; female, 330-650 lb.
- **Life span:** about 25 years in the wild

> Use clip art or photos to make your presentation fun to look at.

Survival in the Arctic

- **Sense of smell:** can smell prey a mile away and even under water
- **Feet:** Covered with fur and small bumps to keep them from slipping on ice
- **Keeping warm:** Two layers of fur and a thick layer of fat protect them from cold

Life Cycle
- Usually mate in April or May
- Cubs born in winter den dug by female
- Cubs usually nurse for two and a half years

Use bullet points on slides to guide your oral presentation.

Behavior
- Usually solitary hunters
- Males may play or play-fight with other males
- Rarely fight seriously except in mating season

Polar Bears and Humans
- Will attack people only when hungry
- Hunted by Arctic natives for meat and fur
- Global warming has reduced habitat

Have a strong conclusion for your presentation.

Personal Narrative

A **personal narrative** tells a true story about an experience in the writer's life, how it made the writer feel, and why it was important.

Parts of a Personal Narrative

- An opening sentence, or lead, that gets the reader's attention
- Several sentences that introduce the topic of the story
- A body that shows events in chronological order, or sequence
- Details and dialogue
- An ending that tells how the story worked out or what the writer learned

Pilgrim for a Day

Beginning
Attention-getting first sentence

I celebrated Thanksgiving last year with the Pilgrims and the Native Americans. Well, actually it was the day after Thanksgiving, and the Pilgrims were really actors in costumes. We were spending the holiday weekend with my aunt and uncle in Boston, and as a special treat they took us out for a day at Plimoth Plantation. It's a big outdoor history

Sentences that clearly show what the story is about

museum in Plymouth, Massachusetts, a short way from where the real Pilgrims had their colonial village.

We left the 21st century behind minutes after Aunt Lynn parked the van. First we walked through a gate in a tall wooden fence called a palisade. Next we followed a path with cows grazing on each side. This brought us

Middle
Describes events in time order

into a village of homes, barns, and shops with thatched roofs. Men and women wearing seventeenth-century clothes were going about their business as if it were 1627.

Other Transitions
Minutes after
First
Next
A while
Then
After lunch
Last

Vivid details about what the narrator saw and heard

We spent a while just looking around and poking into the houses and stores. Then I overcame my shyness and talked to people.

They sound more English than American, and they talk the way English was spoken in the 1600s, but it wasn't hard to understand them. Each actor takes the role of an actual person of the Plymouth colony. We talked with a blacksmith, a farm wife taking goods to market, and a leather worker.

Narrator's personal thoughts, feelings, and opinions

A woman cooking soup in a kettle over a fireplace was the most interesting. She talked about the ingredients in her soup, how she grew them, and how she stored them so that they wouldn't spoil. Her voice turned grim when I asked her about the voyage from England. She described how many people had died, including her own baby. Her story was so sad that I had to remind myself that she was only playing a role, like in a movie!

After lunch, we wandered down the hill to the Wampanoag village. Those were the Indians from the Thanksgiving story. The people in this village are not role players. They are actual Native Americans, though not all are Wampanoags. They talk about their customs and show how their ancestors made things like arrows and canoes.

The last thing we visited was in the town of Plymouth itself. It has the *Mayflower II*, a copy of the ship that brought the real Plymouth colonists to America. The sailors were role-players too. They talked about how they sailed the ship and how they make things like rope and sails.

Ending
Tells what the writer learned

By then we were all tired and ready for some turkey leftovers. But I probably won't think the same way about Thanksgiving ever again. For one thing, the actors at Plimoth Plantation looked puzzled when I asked about "the first Thanksgiving" that they celebrated with the Native Americans. After a while they pretended to figure out that I meant the "harvest festival" they celebrated in 1621. As for the "Pilgrims," they had no idea what I was talking about when I called them that. It turns out that people didn't call the Plymouth colonists by that name until 200 years later!

Biography

A **biography** is a true story of a person's life and achievements.

Parts of a Biography

- Reasons why the subject is worthy of a biography
- Key dates and events in the person's life
- Explanation of how these events affected the subject

Stephen Hawking

Beginning Identifies the subject and a key event or fact about his life

When Stephen Hawking was 21, he was stricken with a terrible nerve sickness called ALS. It is also known as Lou Gehrig's disease, after a famous baseball player who died from it. Nearly everyone who gets ALS dies within two years, but Hawking has lived with it for 49 years. In fact, he has lived to become one of the most famous scientists in the world.

This paragraph gives information about his birth and early life.

Stephen Hawking was born in Oxford, England, on January 8, 1942. His father was a doctor who studied tropical diseases. He urged his bright son to seek a career in science. Stephen decided that medicine and biology weren't exact enough for him, so he turned to math and physics. He entered Oxford University at age 17 and graduated with honors three years later. His goal as a scientist was to study nothing less than the structure of the whole universe! But then he learned that he had ALS. It eventually led to his being confined to a wheelchair and losing the ability to speak.

Middle Describes personal details and events in the person's life

One of his professors urged Stephen to continue his studies despite his disability. In 1965, Hawking married Jane Wilde. His marriage gave him the courage to pursue his career in science. A year later, he became a

Sequence Clues
January 8, 1942
Age 17
Three years later
1965
A year later
During the 1970s and 1980s
1988

professor at Cambridge University in England. He has been a teacher and researcher there ever since. He and his wife eventually had three children.

These paragraphs show what the subject did that made him famous.

Hawking's main work has been with black holes. These are the mysterious objects in space that are so dense that nothing can escape them, not even light, because their gravity is too strong. Hawking proved that the universe could have started as something like a black hole—a single point that contained all the matter in the universe. This work showed how the "Big Bang" theory of how the universe began could be true. He demonstrated that the universe is filled with mini black holes, left over from that Big Bang.

Hawking's work won him many scientific awards during the 1970s and 1980s. Most of his work can be understood only by other scientists. But in 1988, he published *A Brief History of Time: From the Big Bang to Black Holes.* This book explained his ideas to ordinary readers. It became a best seller and made him a public celebrity.

Hawking can speak only with the aid of an electronic device. But that hasn't kept him from making many TV appearances. Besides several interviews, he has appeared on shows like *Star Trek* and *The Simpsons.* He also speaks frequently to wheelchair-bound young people.

Ending Summarizes the subject's life and achievements

Stephen Hawking is still trying to understand how all the known forces of the universe fit together. This was a problem that even the great Albert Einstein couldn't solve. As Hawking has said, "My goal is a complete understanding of the universe, why it is as it is, and why it exists at all."

Fictional Narrative

A **fictional narrative** is a made-up story. A first-person narrator ("I") can tell the story, or a third-person narrator from outside the action can tell the story.

Parts of a Fictional Narrative

- A setting, or place and time where the story occurs
- Characters who have to solve a problem or conflict
- A plot with events that affect the characters in some way

Entertaining Ethan

Beginning
Introodces the characters

"Can I play your game with you?"

Tim quickly clicked the mouse, and the game vanished from the computer screen. "It's not for little kids," he growled at Ethan. Immediately, he was sorry, as Ethan's mouth turned down. "Oh, don't start crying," he said once he saw Ethan's tears.

Tim was stuck. His mom had asked him to entertain his four-year-old cousin Ethan for the afternoon, even though there were a hundred other things he'd rather be doing. "And that doesn't mean sticking him in front of a TV screen," Mom had added.

Middle
Introduces conflict that the main character must solve.

Tim knew that a computer game about zombies and aliens wasn't exactly suitable for Ethan. But just how *did* you keep a four-year-old happy?

Vivid Verbs
Vanished
Sticking
Scrambled
Squirming
Demanded
Stretch
Dragged
Hauled

"Look, what if I tell you a story?"

"Okay," Ethan said. He scrambled onto Tim's lap—just as he must have done when Aunt Chris or Uncle Don told him stories.

These paragraphs contain the rising action of the story.

Tim didn't like it. He also didn't have any story in mind. He started describing the plot of one of his favorite movies. But Ethan got bored and started squirming. He dropped the story and started another, but Ethan didn't understand it any better than he had understood the first.

"Tell me a story about a giant bird," Ethan demanded.

Dialogue lets readers imagine what characters sound like and what each character is feeling.

"I don't *know* any stories about birds!" Tim said. It was only two o'clock, and the afternoon seemed to stretch ahead like a jail sentence.

Then Tim remembered his little-kid toys. He'd wanted to sell them at a sidewalk sale, but Mom had stuck them away in a closet. "Look, how about we build something?" he said.

"Okay," Ethan said, scrambling off Tim's lap.

Tim dragged a cardboard box out of the closet. It was full of wooden pieces with holes in them and wooden fasteners for putting them together. He saw Ethan's eyes get big. "Let's build a power machine!" Ethan said.

This paragraph shows the climax, or the high point of the story.

"Sure," Tim said, and he thought that maybe now he could get back to his computer game.

Then he saw that Ethan was having trouble fitting the pieces together. "Here, let me help you," he said.

"Okay, but I'm the captain!" Ethan said. "You can help, but I get to say how we build the machine."

"Sure," Tim said. He hauled out another box, this one filled with plastic blocks.

"Man, we can build a whole *city!*" Ethan exclaimed.

"Well, let's start with the power machine," Tim said, remembering how much fun he'd had with those toys. "Go on, captain, tell me what we should do."

Ending Shows how the characters solved the conflict.

They were still building when Uncle Don came to pick up Ethan.

"Just give us five more minutes," Ethan begged.

Uncle Don looked at Tim. "Is that okay with you?"

Tim grinned. "You heard the captain. Five more minutes."

Fantasy Story

A **fantasy story** uses magic or other unreal ideas as a main part of the plot, characters, or setting.

Parts of a Fantasy Story

- Characters who have to solve a problem or conflict
- Made up elements that are not like real life
- Themes from traditional myths, legends, or folklore

The Third Test

Beginning
Introduces the conflict

The forest was a maze. The paths seemed to wind and branch off forever without an exit. Several times Trina thought she had found her way out, only to reach another dead end. She heard the roar of a dragon and the groans of things even worse. She might die here. Then her father would remain in the dungeon of the witch-queen Zulora.

A flashback can tell about earlier events.

Trina felt hopeless. She could imagine Zulora laughing in her tower. Trina had struggled to pass the queen's first two tests. She had climbed Mount Evyll, guarded by crazy monkeys with sharp teeth, to bring back the rare and glittering Amethyst Flower jewel. She had traveled deep into the dark and scary cave of Lothar the Dwarf. She had charmed Lothar into giving her the strange jewel that he said would help her pass this third test and defeat the queen. The jewel lay heavy in her pocket, but so far it was useless.

Middle
Shows how character faces problem

Now the path was getting wider. That might mean Trina was near the exit! *Keep turning right*, she thought.

A hiss interrupted her thoughts. Two threatening eyes glowed in the darkness.

Descriptive Adjectives
Hideous
Glittering
Bleak
Fearsome
Inert
Baleful
Trembling

They belonged to a giant cat with horns, and she was the mouse. Trina sprinted away.

This paragraph shows the turning point of the story.

Now she was as far away as ever from getting out. Tired, she sank down on the forest floor. At least the bed of pine needles made it comfortable. She needed to rest. She lay down and closed her eyes. Just a quick nap, and then…

A sound like crystal bells was coming from her apron pocket. She drew out Lothar's jewel. It was glowing! The jewel grew larger in her hands until it was a slab of glass.

Moments later, a map appeared on the glass. It showed a forest and a winding pathway with many branches and dead ends. Here and there were words like "Danger: Dragon," and "Danger: Quicksand." There was a blinking arrow next to words that said, "This way out!"

Ending
Shows how the character solved the conflict

A light was blinking in the center of the glass. Trina wasted no time. She followed the arrow and the blinking light moved with her until she was out of the maze. Queen Zulora's castle lay just ahead, and with the magic map, Trina could defeat the queen and rescue her father.

Note how the author of this piece:

- Used sensory details to make vivid descriptions that the reader can imagine.

  She heard the roar of a dragon and the groans of things even worse.

  She had climbed Mount Evyll, guarded by crazy monkeys with sharp teeth, to bring back the rare and glittering Amethyst Flower jewel.

- Allowed readers to hear the main character's important thoughts.

  Just a quick nap, and then…

Play

A **play** is a story performed by actors in front of an audience. The scenes, dialogue, and characters' actions tell the entire story.

 **Parts of a Play**

- Descriptions of the characters and setting
- Lines of dialogue that tell what each character says
- Stage directions that tell the actors how to move or speak
- Scenery and props that make the scene more realistic

Setting
Tells where and when the play takes place and what the audience sees

Props
Listed at the beginning of the play

Dialogue
Tells what characters say and uses realistic language

The Bus Driver

SCENE ONE (*A school bus, present day. MAC, the driver, is at far stage right. Schoolchildren in the seats bounce and sway. The bus stops suddenly, and they lurch forward in the seats. JENNY, a sixth-grade girl, enters the bus. She wears a backpack and carries a book and a lunch bag. She spots PAM several rows back with an empty seat next to her.*)

JENNY: (*waving*) Hey, Pam!

PAM: (*unhappily*) Oh, hi, Jenny.

JENNY: (*walking toward her*) Listen, you'll never guess—

MAC: (*surly, pointing*) Hey, take that empty seat in the back!

JENNY: But I always sit next to Pam!

MAC: New bus driver, new rules. You sit where I tell you.

JENNY: (*looks at him and shrugs*) Okay.

(*Jenny takes a step toward the back of the bus. Students lurch backward as the bus starts. Jenny loses her balance, and her things fall in the aisle.*)

JENNY: Whoa!

Words that tell actors how to move and to say lines
Bounce and sway
Lurch forward
Waving
Unhappily
Walking toward her
Surly
Pointing
Shrugs
Loses her balance
Shouting
Whispers

(Jenny bends down to gather her things but falls again as other children sway. Pam leans down from her seat to help her.)

JENNY: Assigned seats on a school bus? What's going on? And where's Marty?

PAM: No idea. All I know is, I got on the bus this morning and this guy Mac was driving instead of Marty. He says he's on this route for the rest of the semester.

MAC: *(shouting back)* And no talking!

JENNY: *(whispers)* I'll talk to you at school.

Jenny goes to the back of the bus and sits next to JOSH.)

JOSH: Welcome to the back of the bus.

JENNY: *(whispering)* Shh! You'll make the grouch mad.

JOSH: It's okay. He can't hear us back here. This guy must think he's a prison guard or something.

JENNY: Maybe he just woke up in a bad mood. *(looks through her lunch bag)* Oh, great. Hard-boiled egg's broken.

JOSH: Yeah, he did that on purpose. We should complain to the school.

JENNY: Josh, it's his first day. Let's see what happens.

Note how the author of this piece:

- Ended the first scene of the play with an unresolved conflict.

  JENNY: Josh, it's his first day. Let's see what happens.

  Plays often contain several scenes in which new action takes place, including a final scene, in which the action is resolved.

- Used language to make the dialogue sound like speech real kids would use. The writer uses words like *hey, hi, okay,* and *Whoa!*

Opinion Essay

An **opinion essay** is a composition that presents the writer's personal views about a topic and provides reasons to support the writer's views.

Parts of an Opinion Essay

- An introduction that expresses the writer's opinion
- A short summary and details that back up the opinion
- When relevant, the writer's personal experience
- Reasons that are presented in a logical order
- A summary that contains a suggestion

The Great Flavor Debate

Introduction
States the writer's opinion

There is one question that people ask again and again: "Which ice cream flavor is better: vanilla or chocolate?" All flavors of ice cream are delicious, but this question has a real answer! Chocolate is definitely a better flavor than vanilla.

First, chocolate has more variety. If you go to an ice cream shop, you will see that they offer many varieties of chocolate. An ice cream shop usually has dark chocolate,

Details support the opinion.

milk chocolate, and even white chocolate. Vanilla is just vanilla. The most exciting vanilla gets is those little black specks that don't taste like anything. Chocolate is definitely more exciting.

Second, eating chocolate can be good for your health. Eating small amounts of dark chocolate can be good for your heart. On the

Reasons
Given in order of importance

other hand, because vanilla is expensive, some ice cream has fake vanilla in it. That fake vanilla won't make you sick, but it isn't as good for you as dark chocolate.

Other Transitions
However
With that said
Meanwhile
Additionally
Similarly
Later
Next
Last

Finally, chocolate is a more popular flavor than vanilla. My school has an ice cream station, and we are allowed to get one ice cream treat on Fridays. I have to get to the ice cream station very early because everyone takes the chocolate first. If you wait until the end of the lunch period, the ice cream station will have only vanilla left. This is how I know that most people prefer chocolate. If most people like something, that thing must be very good! Plus, both of my parents prefer chocolate, and so does my brother.

Ice cream is a fantastic treat no matter the flavor, and vanilla can still be exciting if you mix in fruit, like bananas or berries. If you must decide between chocolate and vanilla, though, always choose chocolate. Chocolate is healthier for your heart and has more variety, so it is more exciting. Plus, most people prefer chocolate, so you'll get to share the experience with your friends.

Ending
Contains summary and recommendation

Note how the author of this piece:

- Introduced the essay with a question.

  Another way she could have introduced the essay is to use a quotation or a fact.

  Jo Brand wisely said, "Anything is good if it's made of chocolate.".
  When I surveyed my homeroom class, I found out that 24 out of 30 people like chocolate ice cream better than vanilla.

- Shared personal experiences that supported her opinion.

  I have to get to the ice cream station very early because everyone takes the chocolate first …This is how I know that most people prefer chocolate.

Persuasive Essay

A **persuasive essay** is a composition in which the writer tries to convince the reader to believe the writer's opinion.

Parts of a Persuasive Essay

- An introduction that expresses the writer's position
- A short summary and details that back up the position
- When relevant, the writer's personal experience
- Logical support, offered in a sensible order
- A summary that restates the position

Introduction
Communicates the writer's position

It is important to play a musical instrument. Creating and performing music is good for your brain and fun for you. Everyone should play an instrument. If you don't play one yet, you should learn the piano.

People have loved pianos ever since they were invented. At first, only girls played. A proper lady knew how to play piano and sing. She played to entertain her family and friends. Now, anyone can play. Some people play only for fun. Some people play in competitions to win money or prizes. Others play as their jobs, and they are so good that people pay money to hear them play.

Body
Explains details that support the position

Playing the piano is difficult but rewarding. If you learn to play the piano, you will be better at remembering things you learn in school. This is because piano requires concentration. When you play, you exercise your brain like exercising a muscle when playing a sport. Finally, playing is more active than just sitting and watching TV. When you play piano you still sit, but your mind and fingers are very active.

Logical support is listed in order of importance.

Other Transitions
However
Still
Meanwhile
Additionally
Also
Later
Then
Last

To play the piano, you sit on a wooden bench and put your hands on the 88 black and white keys. It is very hard to play because you don't just make up what notes to hit. You have to read music. Music looks like a lot of black dots on a piece of paper. Learning to read music is like learning another language. If you know how to read music, you can talk to the piano. You can make it sing! You can also write your own music. Then, strangers can play the song you invented!

I have played the piano since I was 5 years old. Piano is very fun for me because when I play it, *I* am the one making music. I sit, I move my fingers, and I get to hear a beautiful song. I play songs written by famous people from the past, such as Beethoven and Debussy. I also play songs from my favorite movies and TV shows. I like playing piano because it makes me feel creative.

Playing piano is one of many options in music, and in my opinion, it is the best. Playing piano is great because it is a healthy, fun hobby. You'll love making beautiful music. Once you start playing piano, you won't want to stop!

Ending
Summarizes the main arguments

Note how the author of this piece:

- Shared a relevant personal experience.

  I have played the piano since I was 5 years old.

- Concluded the essay by summarizing her main arguments. Another way to end a persuasive essay is to include a fact or a description.

  Only 1% of adults play an instrument. If everyone learns to play piano, we can make the world a more musical place.

  Imagine sitting at a piano and putting your hands on the cool, glossy keys. You press down and hear your own sweet melody.

Response to a Play

A **response to a play** is an essay that analyzes the script of a play and states the writer's opinion of it.

Parts of a Response to a Play

- The writer's opinion of the play
- An analysis of the play's characters, plot, and setting
- An opinion of how the text will work as a dramatic performance
- Details from the text that support the writer's opinion

Introduction
States the writer's main idea in a topic sentence

Body
Describes the setting, plot, and main characters

The Junkman's Star Cruise by Frank Maltesi

A science-fiction movie with special effects can make you believe that you're on an alien planet or a future Earth. Can a play, presented live on a stage, bring settings like these to life too? That's the question I asked when I read Frank Maltesi's sci-fi play, *The Junkman's Star Cruise.*

The "junkman" is David Wax, a man who works on a space station in the year 2190. Maltesi's stage directions describe the setting as a plain working world. Scenes take place in labs, offices, and a cafeteria. The only setting that seems out-of-this-world is a small shuttle-like spaceship.

David's boss at the space station is afraid that aliens from another planet will start a war with Earth. David would almost welcome something exciting like that. His two astronaut friends, Janice and Pete, get to explore new planets, but David finds his job boring. He calls himself the junkman because his job is to control a computer that shoots laser beams at garbage that floats through space. He zaps broken satellites and other electronics so that they won't be a danger to space flight. David feels that nothing interesting will ever happen to him.

These sentences establish the conflict.

Then David's computer sees a space probe heading for Earth on a strange flight path. His boss, the strict Dr. Shirley Freed, thinks it's a secret space weapon from a dangerous alien planet. She orders David to destroy the space probe, but he believes it's an alien probe sent to make friendly contact with Earth. To destroy it would mean ruining a chance to learn about a non-human civilization. The second act of the play shows David and his astronaut friends' secret mission to examine the probe, what they discover, and what happens as a result. I won't spoil the ending, but let's just say that by the end of the play David isn't bored anymore.

Details support the author's opinions about the characters and setting.

Maltesi's dialogue brings David, Janice, and Pete to life. They reveal their reasons for wanting to work in space and their common love for adventure. Dr. Freed is a less successful character. She seems like the tough police chief or tough boss from any book, television show, or movie.

The plot and characters make the play interesting, but I have to wonder how it plays on the stage. Maltesi describes the settings in general terms, such as the space station "looking unfinished, like a building under construction" and the view of Earth through a window. Only the probe itself is described in detailed stage directions.

Conclusion Summarizes the writer's point of view and restates the main idea

One of the fun things about reading science fiction is that you can imagination the strange settings. If you are watching a science-fiction movie or a play, though, the set design and special effects need to make you feel like you're there. I would recommend reading *The Junkman's Star Cruise* to anyone who likes science fiction. On the other hand, before I'd recommend seeing the play on the stage, I would have to see if the sets really bring the play to life.

Author Response

An **author response** is an essay about the works of a specific writer. It is not a response to a single book but a report on an author's style as shown by two or more works.

Parts of an Author Response

- Facts about the author and his or her books
- The writer's opinion or point of view about the author

Andrew Clements, Author of Realistic Fantasy

Introduction
Gives the main idea of the essay

Andrew Clements must be young at heart. If not, he has an incredible memory of what it's like to be a kid in school. Most of his books are about school and what goes on between kids and their classmates and teachers. That part of Clements's books is always so realistic that you might not realize that he is often writing fantasy.

Body
Contains details that support the main idea

Take for instance Clements's book *Frindle*, which I read in the fourth grade. The main character of *Frindle*, Nick Allen, is fascinated by words. One day he asks his teacher, Mrs. Granger, where words come from. He wants to know who decides that the animal that barks and wags its tail should be called a dog. The teacher replies, "You do," meaning that a word means whatever the people who speak a language say it means. This gives Nick the idea that if he starts calling a pen a "frindle," maybe he can start a movement to change the word—and he does. By the time

This paragraph explains how the writer's view of the author applies to one book.

Nick's parents and Mrs. Granger get annoyed enough to try to stop it, a pen is called a frindle all over town. When you think about it, you know something like that could never happen. It's no more real than the wizards in *Harry Potter*. But because school is presented in such a realistic way, you can almost believe it. And that's why *Frindle* is fun.

I didn't realize this about *Frindle* until I read Clements's *School Story* this year. Natalie Nelson is a 6th-grade girl who is a really good writer. She lives in New York, where her mother is a children's book editor at a publishing company. Natalie writes a story that is so good that her friend Zoe Reisman talks her into sending it to her mom's company under a fake name. So far *School Story* is completely realistic, even though it's a stretch that a 6th grader could write a book that's good enough to be published. But then *School Story* takes a wacky turn. Zoe poses as an author's agent to try to sell Natalie's book—and gets away with it. When they need an adult to keep the deception going, Zoe talks their teacher, Ms. Clayton, into joining them—and she agrees!

Here, as in *Frindle*, Andrew Clements is stretching the definition of "realistic fiction." When you take a step back and think about what's going on, you *know* that a 12-year-old like Zoe could never get away with impersonating an adult, even by e-mail. Also, can you imagine a teacher behaving like Ms. Clayton and not getting fired? The book is so well set in the world we all know, the world of homework, 6th-grade social life, and busy parents, that the story feels true.

The schools in Andrew Clements's stories are always real places, even when the situations may be a little fantastic—or a lot, like the boy who turns invisible in *Things Not Seen*. His readers may be too young to know much about the world, but we do know school! And so does Andrew Clements.

These paragraphs compare two of the author's books, showing how they both illustrate the writer's main idea.

Conclusion Gives a summary of the main idea

Book Review

A **book review** is an essay that analyzes a book and gives the writer's opinion of it.

Parts of a Book Review

- The writer's thoughts, feelings, and ideas about the book
- An analysis of the book's characters, plot, and setting
- Details and examples from the book that support the writer's opinion

Introduction
Tells what the book is about in two sentences

A topic sentence states the writer's opinion and main idea.

Body
Tells the plot and the writer's opinion

These paragraphs summarize the plot and how the main characters interact.

Johnny Tremain by Esther Forbes

Johnny Tremain is the story of a teen boy whose life changes in unexpected ways. What makes this common subject different is that the book's setting is Boston at the time of the American Revolution. The historical setting and characters bring *Johnny Tremain* to life in interesting ways.

The story begins in 1773. Johnny, a 14-year-old orphan, works for Ephraim Lapham, a silversmith. Johnny is a skilled artist in silver, and he knows it. He brags about his talent and behaves rudely to Mr. Lapham's other workers. Then, Johnny burns his hand in a puddle of hot silver. Since he is no longer useful to the Laphams, he loses his job.

Things go from bad to worse for Johnny. He cannot find a job to make a living, and he does not have a home. Then Johnny meets Rab Silsbee. Rab is a member of the Sons of Liberty, a group of patriots who are protesting against British rule and taxes. Through Rab, Johnny meets historical figures like Samuel Adams and John Hancock. He becomes part of the events that lead to the American Revolution, such as the Boston Tea Party and Paul Revere's ride. The book ends with Johnny joining the Patriot Army.

Details about plot, character, and setting support the writer's opinion.

Esther Forbes presents Johnny's world so realistically that sometimes it's hard to tell which characters and events are real and which are made up. She describes Boston as a city of cobblestone streets, lively sailors, and milkmaids driving cows to the Boston Common (which today still exists as a park). Readers meet imaginary characters like Lydia, an African servant who is secretly a Patriot spy, as well as real people from that time period.

Johnny Tremain is an exciting book with many plot twists. The novel also shows how history changes people. Esther Forbes wrote the book during World War II, when lots of young Americans found their lives suddenly changed by history. For that reason, the book had meaning for readers back then. History is happening around us, too, so Johnny's story has meaning for readers today. That is why I would recommend *Johnny Tremain*.

Conclusion Restates the main idea and the writer's opinion

Note how the author of this piece

- Organized the book review in a logical way, describing the plot in time order and then giving his opinions.

- Gave a positive opinion of the book.

  Another way he could have reviewed the book is to suggest changes to the book.

  Although I enjoyed reading Johnny Tremain, some readers might be confused if they have not yet learned about the American Revolution. The author should have included more background information.

Persuasive Speech

A **persuasive speech** persuades the audience to think or act a certain way. The writer uses logic to support his or her argument.

Parts of a Persuasive Speech

- An introduction that communicates the writer's position
- A short summary and details that back up the position
- When relevant, the writer's personal experience
- Logical support that is offered in a sensible order
- A summary that restates the position

Introduction
Communicates the writer's position

As president of our Student Government, I have called this assembly to address the quality of our school lunches. The lunch served here, while affordable and filling, is not healthy. Every day we eat the same thing: fries and pizza. We must demand better lunches.

Body
Contains details that support the writer's position

If we eat better, we will study better. Think about how you feel after eating five cookies. First, you get overexcited from the sugar. Then, you get really tired. Eating healthy food, however, makes you feel good. You can perform at your best because your body is getting what it needs.

Explain supporting ideas in order of importance.

At this school, the lunches are unacceptable. We get two choices every day, and pizza with fries is always one of them. The other option is usually something kids don't like, so everyone ends up eating pizza. I agree pizza is delicious. However, we cannot eat it so often. We know from health class that a balanced diet is very important. Eating pizza and fries provides some nutrients, but not enough. We need fruits, vegetables, whole grains, and light dairy.

Other Transitions
Yet
Still
Since
Further
Also
After
Then
Finally

When relevant, share your personal experience.

Here is what I imagine: a stocked salad bar with many choices. A salad bar is a good idea because it offers a lot of healthy options. Students will be able to pick exactly what they want. If a student does not like eggs, for example, he or she can skip the eggs and eat other things.

I had a meeting with Principal Ross to talk about all of this. I learned that we do not have healthy food because it is expensive. Principal Ross told me that it is cheaper to serve frozen fries than fresh fruits and vegetables. I know money is a big deal, but I believe health is even more important. So we students must demand better food.

Later today, I will pass around a petition saying we need healthy food options during lunch. Specifically, it suggests a salad bar and freshly cooked meals. When you see the petition, please sign it. Our bodies are important, and our bodies prefer fresh food. So stand up for your health and sign the petition. Demand a salad bar. Demand fresh meals. Demand something other than daily pizza and fries!

Ending Contains a call to action, or words telling the audience what to do

Note how the author of this speech

- Uses *imperative* language—language that tells the audience what we should or must do.

- Other ways the author could have been persuasive are to ask questions or offer statistics.

How do you feel after eating fries? Would you rather eat greasy fries or a crisp pear? Eight out of ten fifth-graders are tired of our school lunches.

Notetaking Strategies

You use **notetaking strategies** whenever you gather information for a report or essay. Taking notes on note cards helps you decide what information to use and how to organize it.

Parts of Notetaking Strategies

- Write one main idea or topic on each card. Add supporting details.
- Write the title, author, and page number or website address of each source you use.

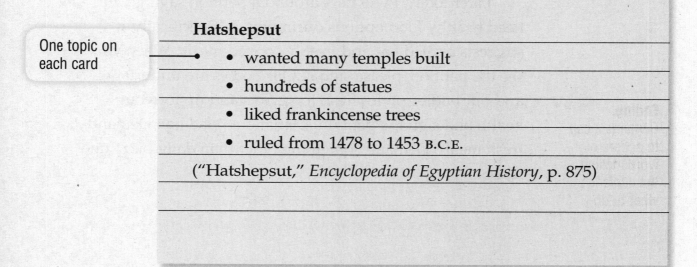

One topic on each card

Hatshepsut
- wanted many temples built
- hundreds of statues
- liked frankincense trees
- ruled from 1478 to 1453 B.C.E.

("Hatshepsut," *Encyclopedia of Egyptian History*, p. 875)

List details under topics they support.

Nefertiti
- wife of Akhenaten (p. 5)
- Akhenaten: pharaoh from 1353 to 1336 B.C.E. (p. 7)
- may have ruled after husband's death (p. 94)

(Robert Amos, *The Great Nefertiti*)

Cleopatra

- was actually Cleopatra VII of Ptolemy (Greek) dynasty that had conquered Egypt
- was 18 when she became queen; for a while shared power with her younger brother
- noted for her intelligence and lively conversation
- ruled 51 to 30 B.C.E.

(Lionel Casson, Ancient Egypt Online)

Topic: Queens of Ancient Egypt

I. Hatshepsut
   A. ruled from 1478 to 1453 B.C.E.
   B. wanted many temples built
   C. liked frankincense trees

II. Nefertiti
   A. wife of Akhenaten
   B. Akhenaten: pharaoh from 1353 to 1336 B.C.E.
   C. may have ruled after husband's death

III. Cleopatra
   A. ruled from 51 to 30 B.C.E
   B. was actually Cleopatra VII of Ptolemy (Greek) dynasty that had conquered Egypt
   C. was 18 when she became queen; for a while shared power with her younger brother

Journal

A writer's **journal** is a place to record experiences, thoughts, dreams, ideas, responses to literature, or anything else that strikes the writer's imagination.

Parts of a Journal Entry

- Date that shows when the entry was written
- Less-formal language than used in an essay; can include sentence fragments and abbreviations

Date of entry

January 8, 2012

A dreary, gray day. I woke up late—it's the last day of vacation! I thought about sending an e-mail to Angus, but instead I went into the attic. Found my old copy of <u>The Phantom Tollbooth</u>. What a great book! I would like to write like Norton Juster.

Here are my New Year's resolutions, a few days late:

1. Clean room more often

2. Go to library weekly

3. Spend less time in front of screens

4. Be a little nicer to Pete, even if he is sometimes the world's worst brother.

A journal is a place to record personal thoughts and feelings as well as experiences.

January 10, 2012

Using figurative language helps you find and develop your writing style.

School started again yesterday. Already I have a mountain of homework to climb. Mr. Hearn assigned us a social studies project. We're supposed to choose any one of the ancient civilizations we studied this semester and write a 2-page paper on why it's the one we'd most like to live in. My choice would be "none of the above." That's not allowed, but who would want to live in any time except now? Who wants to be ruled by a king who thinks he's a god?

From what I've read, none of those places were good for girls and women. And let's not even talk about living without modern conveniences like cars and cell phones.

Hmm, I have to think about this.

January 11, 2012

A bright, clear day for a change. Came right home from school and got out my roller skates for the first time since I don't know when. Went skating on the bike path along the canal, past the stadium and back. It was great exercise and a lot of fun. Also needed time to think about what Clare said at lunch today. She's been my best friend since forever, but I didn't like it when she was talking about other people. Made me wonder who gossips about _me_.

Is it too late to add to my list of New Year's resolutions?

5. <u>Don't gossip!</u>

January 13, 2012

Excited for the weekend! I have important schoolwork to do, though. On Monday, I need to tell Mr. Hearn my choice for the social studies project. I think I'm going to do ancient Egypt.

-Had important queens, like Cleopatra

-Built the pyramids

-Interesting culture

-Egyptian writing

Now that I think about it, ancient Egypt was actually pretty cool. I'm excited about my project now. I'm off to the library to do some research!

It can be fun to review your journal entries later to see how your ideas have changed.

You can use a journal to brainstorm for an essay.

Index

A

Argument Writing
    Argument, 30, 32, 60, 62
    Argument Paragraph, 26
    Book Review, 28
    Opinion Essay, 54
    Persuasive Letter, 58
    Problem-Solution Essay, 56
    Response Paragraph, 24
Author Response, 148

B

Biography, 134
Book Review, 28, 150
Business Letter, 124

C

Cause-Effect Essay, 48, 106
Charts, *See* **Graphs, Diagrams, and Charts**
Checklists and Rubrics, 104
Classification Essay, 36, 116
Common Errors in Writing, *See* **Conventions**
Compare-Contrast Essay, 44, 110
Computer, *See* **Technology**
Conventions, 90

D

Definition Essay, 38, 118
Diagrams, *See* **Graphs, Diagrams, and Charts**
Drafting, 76
Drafting/Revising, 22, 32, 42, 52, 62, 72

E

Editing, 80
Essay
    See Cause-Effect Essay
    See Classification Essay
    See Compare-Contrast Essay
    See Definition Essay
    See Explanation Essay
    See How-to Essay
    See Informational Essay
    See Opinion Essay
    See Persuasive Essay
    See Problem-Solution Essay
    See Procedural Essay
Evaluation, 104
Explanation Essay, 114

F

Fantasy Story, 138
Fictional Narrative, 20, 22, 136
Field Notes, 66
Fluency, *See* **Sentence Fluency**

G

Grammar, Punctuation, and Usage, *See* **Conventions**
Graphic Organizers, 82, *See also* **Prewriting**
Graphs, Diagrams, and Charts, 128

H

How-to Essay, 112
How to Use This Book, 6

I

Ideas, 82
Informative/Explanatory Writing
    Business Letter, 124
    Cause-Effect Essay, 48, 106
    Classification Essay, 36, 116
    Compare-Contrast Essay, 44, 110
    Definition Essay, 38, 118
    Explanation Essay, 114
    Graphs, Diagrams, and Charts, 128
    How-to Essay, 112
    Informational Essay, 40, 42
    Interview, 120
    Multimedia Presentation, 130
    News Story, 122
    Problem-Solution Essay, 46, 108
    Procedural Essay, 34
    Research Report, 50, 52, 125
    Science Observation Report, 125
    Survey: Social Studies, 123
Internet, 94, 96
Interview, 120
Instructions, 112

J

Journal, 156

L

Letter
  See Business Letter
  See Persuasive Letter

M

Models, *See* Writing Models and Forms
Multimedia Presentation, 130

N

Narrative Poem, 64
Narrative Writing
  Biography, 134
  Fantasy Story, 138
  Fictional Narrative, 20, 22, 136
  Field Notes, 66
  Narrative Poem, 64
  Personal Narrative, 16, 70, 72, 132
  Personal Narrative Paragraph, 14
  Play, 140
  Radio Script, 68
  Story Scene, 18
News Story, 112
Notetaking, 100
Notetaking Strategies, 154

O

Opinion Essay, 54, 142
Opinion Writing
  Author Response, 148
  Book Review, 150
  Opinion Essay, 142
  Persuasive Essay, 144
  Persuasive Speech, 152
  Response to a Play, 146
Organization, 88

P

Paragraph
  See Argument Paragraph
  See Personal Narrative Paragraph
  See Response Paragraph
Peer Review, *See* Writing Process
Personal Narrative, 14, 16, 70, 72, 132
Persuasive
  Essay, 144
  Letter, 58
  Speech, 152
Play, 140
Poem, *See* Narrative Poem
Practical Writing, 154, 156
Presentation, *See* Publishing
Prewriting, 20, 30, 40, 50, 60, 70, 76
Problem-Solution Essay, 46, 56, 108
Procedural Essay, 34
Prompt, *See* Writing to a Prompt
Proofreading, *See* Editing
Publishing, 81
Purposes for Writing, 8

R

Radio Script, 68
Research, 98, 100
Research Report, 50, 52, 125
Response Paragraph, 24
Response to a Play, 156
Revising, 78
Rubrics, 104

S

Science Observation Report, 125
Sentence Fluency, 88
Sequence, *See* Narrative Writing
Social Studies, 123
Story Scene, 18
Strategies, *See* Notetaking Strategies, *See also* Writing Strategies

T

Technology, 94, 96
Test Prep, 102
The Writing Process, 10
The Writing Traits, 12

V

Voice, 86

W

Web, *See* Internet
Writing for the Web, 96
Writing Models and Forms
    Argument, 30, 32, 60, 62
    Argument Paragraph, 26
    Author Response, 148
    Biography, 134
    Book Review, 28, 150
    Business Letter, 124
    Cause-Effect Essay, 48, 106
    Classification Essay, 36, 116
    Compare-Contrast Essay, 44, 110
    Definition Essay, 38, 118
    Explanation Essay, 114
    Fantasy Story, 138
    Fictional Narrative, 20, 22, 136
    Field Notes, 66
    Graphs, Diagrams, and Charts, 128
    How-to Essay, 112
    Informational Essay, 40, 42
    Interview, 120
    Multimedia Presentation, 130
    Narrative Poem, 64
    News Story, 122
    Opinion Essay, 54, 142
    Personal Narrative, 16, 70, 72, 132
    Personal Narrative Paragraph, 14
    Persuasive Essay, 144
    Persuasive Letter, 58
    Persuasive Speech, 152
    Play, 140
    Practical Writing, 154–156
    Problem-Solution Essay, 46, 56, 108
    Procedural Essay, 34
    Radio Script, 68
    Research Report, 50, 52, 125
    Response Paragraph, 24
    Response to a Play, 146
    Science Observation Report, 125
    Story Scene, 18
    Survey: Social Studies, 123
Writing Process
    Drafting, 74
    Editing, 81
    Prewriting, 76
    Publishing, 81
    Revising, 78
Writing Strategies,
    See Writing Process
    See Writing Traits
    See Writing Workshop
Writing to a Prompt, 102
Writing Traits
    Conventions, 90
    Ideas, 82
    Organization, 84
    Sentence Fluency, 88
    Voice, 86
    Word Choice, 87
Writing Workshop, 92